TIMELESS BIOGRAPHIES

# India's Paralympians

# India's Paralympians

Illustrated by

Mistunee Chowdhury

HARPERCOLLINS
CHILDREN'S BOOKS

First published in India by HarperCollins *Children's Books* 2025
An imprint of HarperCollins *Publishers*
HarperCollins *Publishers* India, Cyber City, Building 10-A, Gurugram, Haryana-122002, India
www.harpercollins.co.in

2 4 6 8 10 9 7 5 3 1



P-ISBN: 978-93-6989-674-5
E-ISBN: 978-93-6989-421-5

Every effort has been made to ensure that the most significant moments in every sportsperson's journey have been covered in the book. However, owing to limitations, some may have been excluded. The facts and milestones of the various athletes presented have been verified as of 30 June 2025 to the best extent possible. While every effort has been made to ensure the accuracy of the details for the sportspersons represented in this book, the publishers are not in any way liable for any inadvertent omissions or errors.

The contents of this book are for informative purposes only. The illustrations produced in this book are an artistic representation meant to enhance the experience of the reader. Neither the illustrator nor the publisher provides a warranty of any kind on the accuracy or veracity of these illustrations.



Typeset in 11/16.8 Newsreader 14pt at
HarperCollins *Publishers* India

Printed and bound at
Nutech Print Services - India

HarperCollins *Publishers*, Macken House, 39/40 Mayor Street Upper, Dublin 1, D01 C9W8, Ireland

# Contents

# Foreword

In every era, there are changemakers who refuse to be defined by limitations—individuals who prove that courage, determination and belief in oneself can push through the harshest barriers. Paralympians are among the most powerful examples of this spirit.

As India's first woman Paralympic medalist, and someone who has lived this journey with chest below paralysis for over 25 years as a para-athlete, an administrator, an advocate and a social worker, I know that sport is more than just competition. For people with disabilities, it can be a path to visibility, dignity and self-worth. It can be the difference between being told what you cannot do and discovering what you can.

This book, *India's Paralympians*, brings together the stories of extraordinary athletes who have made a mark at the highest levels of international sport. The Paralympic Games are one of the most competitive and demanding global sporting events, parallel to the Olympics. Every athlete featured in this book is not just inspiring; they are *elite athletes*, among the best in the world in their disciplines. They train, persevere, and perform with the same intensity, skill and excellence as any top-tier sportsperson.

Each chapter is a window into an athlete's unique journey: the small-town origins, the tryst with disability, the quiet dreams, the setbacks that could have ended it all—and the grit and perseverance that changed everything. These stories matter because representation matters. When young children, with and without disabilities, read about people who look like them, live like them and yet achieve the extraordinary, it changes what they believe is possible.

As someone who has had the privilege of contributing to the evolution of India's para sport ecosystem firsthand, first as an athlete and later as an administrator; I can say with pride that we are at a turning point. Para sports in India are no longer on the margins, they are mainstream, with record-breaking performances, world-class coaching, government support and growing spectatorship and fanbase. We are seeing a surge in talent, greater recognition and a national sentiment that is shifting from sympathy to celebration. But we still have a long road ahead.

Books like this play a vital role in accelerating that change. By including para-athletes in school libraries, classrooms, and bedtime reading, we are telling future generations that disability is not tragedy—it is a facet of human diversity. We are nurturing empathy, respect and the idea that excellence comes in many forms.

To every reader picking up this book: know that you are holding in your hands the lived proof that impossible is just a word. These athletes are not defined by their disability alone. They are defined by discipline, talent and an unshakeable will to rise.

Let these stories move you. Let them challenge your assumptions. And most importantly, let them inspire you to reach higher, no matter what your starting point may be. Happy Reading!

**- Dr Deepa Malik**

Padma Shri, Khel Ratna & Arjuna Awardee
1st Indian Woman Paralympic Medalist
Executive Board Member - Asian Paralympic Committee
Former President – Paralympic Committee of India

# Introduction

Parasports have existed for as long as there have been organized sports events. All the way back in the nineteenth century, when sports and athletics associations were cropping up all over Europe and the United States of America, sporting events for disabled athletes were being held in small capacities, primarily by hospitals and charities. There is evidence of sports clubs for deaf athletes existing as far back as 1888 in Germany.

In 1911, a 'Cripples Olympiad' was organized in the United States, which saw wide participation of athletes from Europe as well. This was the first instance of a large-scale competition organized for people with disabilities. In the early years of the Olympics itself, there was no classification or disbarring of athletes based on their ability, and so the first few editions saw the participation of amputee athletes like German-American George Eyser in 1904, who won multiple medals, and Hungarians Olivér Halassy and Károly Takács. The Games continue to not have any specific ability-wise classification for athletes.

As the popularity of the Olympics grew over the years, its credo of athletic competition–immortalized by the founder of the modern Olympics Pierre de Coubertin's words, 'The important thing in life is not the triumph but the struggle, the essential thing is not to have conquered but to have fought well'–sought to encompass and unite people from all walks of life and abilities in a fair contest. Following World War II, German doctor Ludwig Guttmann, who worked at the Stoke Mandeville Hospital in Buckinghamshire, England, decided to organize a sporting event for veterans with spinal cord injuries to coincide with the 1948 Olympic Games in London. These were called the Stoke Mandeville Games, which then became the International Stoke Mandeville Games when Dutch ex-servicemen and women became a part of it in 1952.

Soon, the scope of the event grew much beyond its original mission of rehabilitation and recreational sport for injured veterans. From the Stoke Mandeville Games emerged its modern offspring, the Paralympics, in 1960, with an expanded roster that included several categories. These have increased through the decades to become more inclusive towards other differently-abled persons than just amputees and paraplegics. Since 1960, the Paralympics are held in tandem with the Olympics, sharing the same host city.

In 1989, the International Paralympic Committee (IPC), a non-profit organization headquartered in Düsseldorf, Germany, was founded in order to better organize the Games as well as support and fund other regional and international parasports events such as the World Para Athletics Championships (previously known as the IPC Athletics World Championships), Asian Para Games, European Para Championships and many more. With 183 National Paralympic Committees represented, it is the biggest organization that supports several disabilities and sports.

And just as every Olympics ceremony begins with the Olympic torch relay that starts from Olympia, the seat of the ancient Olympiads, the Paralympics ceremony begins with the ceremonial lighting of the torch at the Stoke Mandeville Hospital, from where Dr Guttmann had successfully flagged off an event representing all abilities and peoples.

# Classification for Paralympics

The first Stoke Mandeville Games in 1948 featured wheelchair-bound veterans competing in the sport of archery. Since then, the scope of the Paralympics has only grown, with multiple events held across multiple days for different kinds of abilities. To promote the spirit of fair competition and to herald the achievements of athletes, different classifications were put in place over the years. This often results in multiple categories for one sporting event, as well as different equipment for these events.

The IPC has established ten categories for disabilities, including physical, visual and intellectual impairments. Athletes with any one of these can participate in the Paralympics, although not all sports cater to all categories. In broad terms, the disability classifications are as follows:

1. **Physical Impairment:** Within the category of physical impairment, there are eight sub-categories, namely:
    1. Impaired muscle power: limb use affected due to insufficient force generated by the muscles (e.g. resulting from post-polio syndrome or spinal cord injuries).
    2. Impaired passive range of movement: reduced range of movement in one or more joints (e.g. the knee or elbow or wrist cannot function to the best of their ability, resulting in decreased flexibility).
    3. Limb deficiency: partial or complete absence of bones or joints due to either trauma (accident or violence), illness or congenital (from birth) limb deficiency.
    4. Leg-length difference: significant bone shortening of the leg due to congenital deficiency or trauma.

5. Short stature: standing height impacted due to musculoskeletal deficiency of bones or cartilage in the arms, legs and trunk.
6. Hypertonia: increased muscle tension that makes it difficult to stretch or move a muscle (e.g. cerebral palsy).
7. Ataxia: muscle coordination is difficult (cerebral palsy, multiple sclerosis and similar nervous system conditions).
8. Athetosis: inability to maintain symmetrical posture, as well as unbalanced and involuntary limb movement.

2. **Visual impairment:** This includes the impairment of one or more components of the visual system (receptors, visual cortex, optic nerves, eye structure). The athletes can be either partially blind, sufficient to be judged legally blind, or have complete blindness. For those athletes competing in events which require a sighted guide, the two individuals are considered a team and compete as such.
3. **Intellectual disability:** This category includes athletes with significant intellectual impairment or associated impairments that limit adaptive behaviour. This means that the athletes have difficulty understanding or grasping concepts or ideas that can be complex, and have a lot of difficulty in learning new things. While the IPC primarily serves athletes with physical disabilities and impairments, the Paralympics have added intellectual disability as a category with a few clauses, the major one being that the intellectual impairment should be diagnosed before the age of eighteen. For a majority of intellectually disabled athletes, the Special Olympics World Games, which are recognized by the International Olympic Committee (IOC), are held.

## DISCIPLINE-WISE CLASSIFICATION

As more and more impairments and disabilities are added to the Paralympics list, there has also been a call over the past decade to create a 'functional classification', which has resulted in the current classification system used by IPC as well as other regional parasports committees. This allows for athletes with different impairments to compete against each other. Rather than examine a specific impairment, a functional classification is conducted by a panel of medical and technical experts, who examine an athlete's functional abilities in terms of coordination, movement and balance and then allot them a category. The category is designated by a letter (usually of the sport or discipline) and a number.

Here are a few of the categories at major Paralympic events:

**Archery:**

1. Open class Recurve Archery: This category consists of shooting from a standing position of 70 m at a 122 cm target made up of ten concentric circles.
2. Open class Compound Archery (for archers with little strength in the arms): In this category, archers will shoot from a sitting position at a distance of 50 m at an 80 cm five-ring target.
3. W1 (compound archery with a bow limited to 20 kg in draw weight and without magnifying sights): This category consists of quadriplegic archers with an impairment in the lower limbs, trunk and one arm; they shoot from 50 m at a ten-band 80 cm target.

**Para Athletics:**

In athletics, athletes are classified by the letter T for Track or F for Field depending on their choice of discipline. The numbering for athletes follows the code below:

1. 11–13: Vision impairment.
2. 20: Intellectual impairment.
3. 31–38: Co-ordination impairments.
4. 40–47: Short stature, upper limb competing with prosthesis or equivalent, lower limb competing with prosthesis or equivalent.
5. T51–54: Wheelchair races.
6. F51–58: Seated throws.
7. 61–64: Lower limb competing with prosthesis.

**Badminton:**

The following are the classifications for para badminton at the Paralympics. The letters 'WH' stand for wheelchair athletes, 'SL' for standing/lower and 'SU' for standing/upper, with the second letter indicating the location of the limb impairment. 'SH' stands for standing/short stature.

1. WH1: Athletes using a wheelchair with severely impaired leg and trunk function.
2. WH2: Athletes using a wheelchair with minor impairments to leg and trunk function.
3. SL3: Athletes competing standing with a lower limb impairment and balance problems in walking or running.
4. SL4: Athletes competing standing with less severe impairment than in SL3; they demonstrate lower limb impairment and minor balance problems in walking or running.
5. SU5: Athletes with impairment of the upper limbs; the impairment could be in the playing or non-playing hand.
6. SH6: Short stature and standing athletes.

**Judo:**

Para judo is a visually disabled sport, and as such, consists of two main categories:

1. J1: Those with complete blindness.
2. J2–3: Those with a significant vision impairment and a field of vision less than 60 degrees.

After this initial categorization, para judokas are classified into different weight classes.

**Swimming:**

Swimmers are classified primarily on the basis of their impairment, as well as the style they employ. In the classification, 'S' denotes swimming, specifically butterfly, backstroke and crawl, 'SB' denotes swimming breaststroke, while 'SM' denotes multi-swimming events. The various categories are thus as follows:

1. S1–S10/SB1–SB9/SM1–SM10: Physical impairment

   The greater the number, the less severe the swimmer's limitation(s). Para swimmers with different impairments may compete against one other as classes are allocated based on the impact the impairment has on swimming, rather than on the impairment itself.

2. S/SB/SM11–13: Vision impairment

   11: Includes swimmers with extremely low visual sensitivity and/or no light perception. They must wear blackened goggles during races to ensure fair competition.

   12: Consists of swimmers with a higher visual sensitivity than those competing in the S/SB11 sport class and/or a visual field of less than 10 degrees (an unimpaired field of vision is about 170–180 degrees).

   13: This contains para swimmers with the least severe vision impairment eligible for Paralympic sport. They have the highest visual clarity and/or a visual field of less than 40 degrees.

3. S/SB/SM14: Intellectual impairment

   This category includes swimmers with an intellectual impairment, which typically leads to them having difficulties with pattern recognition and memory, or having a slower reaction time, impacting sport performance in general.

**Table Tennis:**

Para-table tennis consists of eleven classes in total (five sitting, six standing):

1. TT1–5: Wheelchair athletes
2. TT6–10: Standing athletes
3. TT11: Athletes with intellectual impairments

Table tennis players who have difficulty gripping the racket may use orthotics to attach the racket to the hand or use strapping to maintain their grip of the racket handle only.

**Shooting:**

Para shooters are broadly classified into two categories, following which they are further classified based on their choice of arms, i.e., pistol or rifle.

1. SH1: Includes shooters who are able to hold their gun without difficulty and shoot from a standing or sitting position (in a wheelchair or chair). SH1 athletes may use a pistol or a rifle.
2. SH2: Includes shooters who are unable to hold their rifle independently, so use a stand, but can aim by themselves and control the rifle when they shoot. Certain athletes may have an assistant to reload their gun.

# Archery

IND

## Harvinder Singh

### RECURVE ARCHERY

It had started drizzling soon after the wind picked up. The other competitor in the match, South Korea's Kim Min Su, had just shot an 8 for his final attempt, putting him in a comfortable position. Scored on a scale from 1 to 10, with 10 denoting the rare bullseye, an 8 at such a crucial juncture put the onus on Kim's opponent, India's Harvinder Singh. The archer had to shoot a 9 to win the bronze medal. And now that there was wind and rain, his coaches had told him to stick to attempting a 9 or an 8. Go for the safe shot, they said.

But Harvinder Singh is not one to go for the safe option. He had missed a 10 in an earlier round that had led to him fighting for a bronze rather than a silver or a gold. He took a deep breath, aimed and shot his arrow.

It was a perfect 10. A smile erupted across Harvinder's face as he won the bronze at the Tokyo 2020 Paralympics—the first Indian to ever win a Paralympic medal in archery.

Born in Kaithal, Haryana, in 1991, Harvinder came from a predominantly agricultural family. After contracting an illness shortly after his first birthday, Harvinder was mistakenly given the wrong injection, which resulted in his left leg being impaired. Having grown up in this way, Harvinder didn't know any other way of living, and from an early age engaged in all sorts of physical activities on his family farm.

Having concentrated most of his childhood on his studies, Harvinder was academically gifted. But that was not going to be his calling. He had always been interested in sports, but like most children his age, Harvinder mainly played and watched cricket and hockey.

It was the 2012 Olympics that changed everything. Harvinder saw the magnificence of the sport of archery and knew that he had fallen in love with it. A student of economics at Punjabi University, Patiala, Harvinder took to compound archery like a duck to water and was winning medals in no time. He took his game to the national level and repeated his successes. But that wasn't enough for Harvinder, who simply loved a challenge.

Compound archery uses a system of pulleys and holds that makes the bow easier to use and lighter to lift as compared to recurve archery. Some compound bows come with added sighting devices and thanks to the cams or wheels at the ends of the bow, it is easier to store energy and increase accuracy. It is also for this reason that compound archery is not a discipline at the Olympics, even though it has been one at the Paralympics.

Recurve archery, in contrast, uses a heavier bow, with its limbs drawn back through the strength of a tight string. It is more akin to the old-fashioned bows of yore. But when it comes to the sport, one element of recurve archery is the stance, which puts considerable weight on the opposite leg. For Harvinder, this was his left leg. With his long-time coach Jiwanjot Singh Teja, Harvinder reworked his stance, putting more pressure on his right leg and standing in a way that led to a more balanced posture while shooting.

Armed with this new approach, Harvinder stormed the archery recurve nationals, quickly becoming India's best recurve archer in no time. However, it was in 2018 that his biggest test would arrive: the Asian Para Games, Harvinder's first time in the international arena. But disaster struck right before he left for the Games.

Harvinder's mother, who had always encouraged her son to pursue everything that made him happy and cheered him on for his sporting and educational exploits, passed away mere weeks before the Games were to begin. Although heartbroken, Harvinder did not think of dropping out, knowing that his mother would have wanted him to go to Jakarta for the tournament.

There, in his first international tournament and still reeling from the loss of his mother, Harvinder won the gold. What was more astounding was the dominant nature of his wins, which made him appear a veteran in a sport he had picked up only a few years ago. Harvinder beat his Chinese opponent 6-0 in the final to clinch the gold. He also beat Kim in the semi-finals, foreshadowing his first Paralympics triumph in 2020.

But if you thought that was it, Harvinder was just getting started. Upon winning the bronze and becoming the first Indian archer to win a medal at the Paralympics, his sights were on the gold in the 2024 Summer Games. While the Games started on a promising note, Harvinder qualified ninth for the recurve event, which was much lower than anyone, even Harvinder himself, had anticipated. This knocked his confidence a bit, but as it was before, there was everything still to play for.

Harvinder easily defeated his Polish opponent in straight sets to land the gold and claim legendary status.

Following a lacklustre qualifying round, Harvinder was almost flawless in the remainder of the event en route to his gold. He beat Poland's Lukasz Ciszek in straight sets, bettering his tally and shooting more 10s than he ever had before. In the span of a day, he turned into a household name and the undisputed world champion.

While Harvinder has gone back to preparing for the next Paralympics with the hope of defending his title, there's one other challenge he is aiming to conquer, which he had put on hold after his 2018 win. As an economics student, Harvinder is hoping to finally defend his thesis on labour reforms soon and earn his PhD. Talk about a man of many talents!

# Know More ...

Archery was one of eight original sports that were part of the inaugural 1960 Paralympics, along with being the sport that started the Para sports movement with the 1948 Stoke Mandeville Games.

But did you know about Dartchery? It is exactly what it sounds like—a mix of archery and darts, where the target is a dart board instead of a standard archery target, and the scoring method is exactly like darts!

It was played in pairs from the 1960 Paralympics to the 1980 Games, after which it was discontinued. The United States was the most successful nation in the sport, winning two golds and two silvers, while the erstwhile nation of Rhodesia took one gold to be the second-most successful one.

## Rakesh Kumar

**COMPOUND ARCHERY**

The town of Katra in Jammu is mostly known for the famed shrine of Shri Mata Vaishno Devi, which is also an important source of income for most of the town. Beyond Vaishno Devi, however, the town hadn't made headlines, until now. And it all begins with one of its own sons who has been making waves for quite a few years.

Rakesh Kumar was born in Katra in 1985 to a family that plied its trade in carpentry. Throughout his youth, Rakesh would accompany his father and help him out with his work. This early exposure to handicraft and using fine and heavy tools made Rakesh extremely dextrous and adept with both his hands. This dexterity would also take him to his vocation of choice, which he hoped would be a game changer in the lives of his family, which had been struggling financially for quite some time. That vocation was plumbing.

Soon after he became a plumber, however, disaster struck in 2009. Rakesh was returning from a visit to his aunt's village when the shared cab he was travelling in met with a serious accident. The months that followed were concentrated on recovery and hospitalizations, and the seriousness of his injuries meant that Rakesh wouldn't be able to use his legs again.

While this was a life-altering event, Rakesh's main concern remained his family. His only thought after he had regained consciousness and understood the truth of the situation was that he could neither help his father anymore, nor be a plumber. What hit him much worse in the coming days was the thought that he had become a burden on his family. Rather than him helping them out, they were having to care for him.

But his family did not think so. They rallied around Rakesh and—dipping into their savings—got him a second-hand wheelchair. They even rented a shop near the Vaishno Devi shrine, which would allow Rakesh to eke out a living selling mobile accessories. Trying to keep out the negative thoughts that were swimming around in his mind, Rakesh threw himself into his work, even though it was nowhere near as fulfilling as plumbing.

It was almost seven years later that Rakesh was spotted by archery coach Kuldeep Vedwan, who was on his way to the shrine. Seeing Rakesh's quickness with his hands and his significant upper body strength, Vedwan suggested to him that he should train as an archer. Rakesh was not interested in the sport initially, as his family's financial situation still consumed most of his thoughts. Coincidentally, the Shri Mata Vaishno Devi Shrine Board had only recently opened a sports centre that aimed at training the youth in various disciplines and inculcating a sense of self-belief and physical well-being. Rakesh, on Vedwan's insistence and his family's encouragement, was one of its earliest trainees.

The interest grew, slowly and steadily, till Rakesh had to ask his brother to take care of the shop as he would be at the sports complex from seven in the morning to seven in the evening. His training soon bore fruit, as he debuted on the international stage in 2018 at the Nove Mesto Para Archery tournament in the Czech Republic, where he won a silver in the team tournament. His first Paralympics in Tokyo followed in 2020; this went without any medals, but Rakesh was being noticed by athletes all over the world now.

From a vocation in plumbing to becoming one of the world's best compound archers, it has been quite a journey for Rakesh Kumar.

While the sport gave him joy and provided Rakesh with a sense of accomplishment, he still knew that he had to concentrate on his shop. A huge fan of cricket, and especially Sachin Tendulkar, Rakesh believed that it was the only sport that could actually be considered a job since it literally changed people's fortunes. But now that he was being noticed and was winning medals internationally, including an individual gold at the 7th Fazza Para Archery World Ranking Tournament in 2021, Rakesh noticed a marked change in his situation and for the first time, saw archery as something he could commit to full time. The Katra Sports Complex helped him out with equipment, as well as providing him with the support that he needed. Rakesh soon started training the younger athletes at the complex, earning himself the role of an assistant coach.

The next big change happened in 2022, when Rakesh was paired with fellow Jammu archer Sheetal Devi. Sheetal's youth and vigour complimented Rakesh's steely resolve and will, and the two instantly became an iconic pair in the sport. And it didn't take long for their chemistry to bear fruit. At the Asian Para Games in Hangzhou in 2023, the two won the gold, breaking the world record for the highest score achieved in mixed doubles for Para archery. This partnership also enhanced Rakesh's individual game, where he won the silver quite comfortably. The following year, at the World Para Archery Championships, the pair won the gold again.

Fresh from his latest exploits at the 2024 Paris Paralympics, where he and Sheetal won the bronze, Rakesh has become the talk of his hometown. But he always ensured that due credit was given to his coach Vedwan and his partner and protégée Sheetal. After having secured his family's comfort and future, he is looking towards the next tournament where he can do what he does best.

# Know More ...

While wheelchair football, basketball, volleyball and rugby are well-known wheelchair-based para sports, did you know about Boccia?

Unlike the other aforementioned sports, Boccia is a game of strategy and precision, similar to bowling. Individuals or teams of two to three players take turns getting close to a white ball, called the jack, by tossing, moving or rolling the balls allotted to them, and the one that is closer to the jack gets more points. Each round, called an 'end', consists of six balls, or six throwing opportunities. The team with the most points after four ends wins the game!

## Sheetal Devi

**COMPOUND ARCHERY**

When it comes to sports that use targets, the bullseye is what all athletes are going after. Even if they do not always end up winning, a perfect score shows that they did their best. And while we may not see perfect scores for an attempt at the Olympics or in World Championships, the hard work that goes into it is unparalleled.

Another aspect of sports that involve shooting or aiming is the importance of hand-eye coordination, as well as having an iron grip so that your aim is steady. Now think of doing all this without any hands. Sounds impossible? Meet Sheetal Devi, an archer who constantly defies every single expectation.

Sheetal was born in 2007 in the town of Kishtwar in Jammu. Diagnosed with the congenital condition of phocomelia, her arms remained underdeveloped from birth. But that has never been an obstacle for the young athlete. Growing up in the hills and among the verdant greenery of Jammu, Sheetal has always been an adventurous person, revelling in the outdoors and playing with her friends.

It was at the age of fourteen that her talents were discovered and Sheetal discovered her true calling as well. In the hope of having her own prosthetic arms, Sheetal came to Bengaluru for treatment. Once there, however, she realized that the endeavour was doomed, and after all, Sheetal's strength lay in her legs, which she had used to do everything throughout her life so far.

In Bengaluru, Sheetal met Preethi, who became a mentor and introduced her to para athletes as well as para sports. Upon undergoing a sports assessment with a physiotherapist, it was established that Sheetal, with her immense core strength, was ideal for archery. With that, the budding sportsperson decided to relocate to Katra and begin her training in earnest.

What followed was a period of relentless and considerable training for Sheetal. While her coaches Kuldeep Vedwan and Abhilasha Chaudhry had worked with para athletes and archers before, there are very few archers in the world that shoot with their feet. Fortunately, they had a reference point in the legendary Matt Stutzman, who holds the world record for the longest accurate distance shot ever made by an archer. Stutzman uses his legs and feet for archery, and it was his technique that Sheetal and her coaches studied to come up with a style that would suit her.

In less than a year, Sheetal was competing with other archers on a national level. And it was only a matter of time before the international stage beckoned to her. Sheetal made her international debut in 2023 at the World Para Archery Championships held in Plzeň. There, Sheetal won a silver and became the first female armless archer to win a medal at the event. It was there that she also finally met her role model Matt Stutzman, who was only too happy to interact with her and help her better her stance and shooting.

Sheetal and her archery partner Rakesh Kumar were awarded the Arjuna Award for their exploits in compound archery.

At the 2023 Asian Para Games in Hangzhou, Sheetal became the only female archer in the world to shoot with her feet. And that wasn't her only achievement–in her first two doubles events, she won the gold and silver respectively alongside fellow compatriots Rakesh Kumar and Sarita. Being alongside them gave her confidence and allowed her to showcase her skills. But her legendary status was confirmed at the women's individual event.

Sheetal started off well, but then whether it was nerves or just adapting to the occasion, she found herself trailing at the end of the first three rounds. The competition was close, so Sheetal was not out of it yet, but her next two attempts needed her to be perfect.

And she was perfect. Sheetal landed an astounding six consecutive 10s to win the gold over Singapore's Nur Syahidah Alim. This incredible haul of three medals catapulted Sheetal to the top of the rankings and earned her the crowd's adulation. In one year, she had managed to learn a sport and become the best at it in the world.

In January of 2024, Sheetal was felicitated with the Arjuna Award in recognition of her meteoric rise. At her first Paralympic Games in Paris in the same year, she became the youngest athlete to compete in women's para archery at the age of seventeen. Sheetal won the bronze with her longtime archery partner Rakesh Kumar, adding to a list of accolades that doesn't seem to be ending anytime soon.

# Badminton

# Pramod Bhagat

## SL3 BADMINTON

The village of Shubhai was dead silent, except for the sound of one large speaker in the village chaupal. But the speaker was not emitting much sound either, apart from the constant 'whoosh' or a foreign voice announcing numbers. Most of the villagers did not even understand what was being said, but they were enthralled to see one of their own on the screen. Suddenly the action stopped and the person announcing declared, 'Match, Bhagat.'

The entire village erupted in joy. 2020 had been a year full of loss and fear due to the pandemic, but now it felt like celebrations had finally returned to Shubhai. Everyone, young and old, was dancing in joy at the happy fact that a son of the village had made his name in the world. Soon everyone was being accosted by the sarpanch, who was beaming and distributing sweets across the chaupal, exclaiming, 'Our son has won gold!'

At one corner of the chaupal, where most of the crowd went to celebrate and congratulate, were four people who had as much of a claim on the gold as the champion on screen. They were the four parents of Pramod Bhagat, India's badminton sensation. But four? Well, Pramod's story is anything but usual.

Pramod Bhagat was born in 1988 in Attabira in Odisha. With five other kids, the Bhagat house always seemed to be full, and there was never a moment of silence. The family, although poor, loved each other, and Pramod and his siblings played and stayed together almost all the time. However, at the age of five, Pramod contracted polio, which significantly weakened his left leg. He had to learn and adapt to a new way of moving about, which meant several hours with specialists. While they loved him dearly, his family was in no position to support and take care of him financially. So, Pramod was sent to live in Bhubaneswar with his aunt and uncle, who became his second set of parents.

With his uncle, Pramod discovered a new life and new worlds. At the age of thirteen, his uncle took him to watch a badminton match. As he watched it, Pramod realized that he had never been so engrossed in anything as he was in this sport. He shared this interest with his uncle, who saw the passion the young boy had for the sport and started training him. He was a natural athlete, picking up the game in days and quickly becoming adept at it, despite the obvious difficulty involved. Encouraged by everyone around him who also pitched in to support his dream, Pramod entered a badminton tournament at the age of fifteen to test himself.

While Pramod did not end up winning the tournament, he did end up amazing people with his skills. After a few more events, Pramod won a district-level tournament against able-bodied opponents, an unheard of achievement. This extraordinary feat brought him in contact with S.P. Das, who would become his coach and help him transition into a professional athlete. Having learnt badminton as an outdoor sport, it was quite a surprise for Pramod to find out that it was an indoor event. But following a few initial hurdles and adaptation, he was all ready for the big leagues.

While other athletes are gradually eased into international tournaments, Pramod and his coach believed that they were ready for the second biggest stage that the sport can offer. And so, Pramod's first major event was the 2007 IBAD (International Badminton Association for Disabled) Para-Badminton World Championships. Their belief was proven right when Pramod won the bronze medal on his international debut in the singles as well as doubles categories.

With this experience in his pocket, there was no other way to go for Pramod but up. In 2009, at his second IBAD Para-Badminton World Championship in Seoul, he won the gold. Not just that, Pramod's final match was against the same player who had bested him two years prior. Thailand's Subpong Meepian had managed to win a one-sided bout in the 2007 IBAD Para-Badminton World Championships at both the individual and doubles level. But in 2009, Pramod dismantled him 21-10 21-13, announcing his legend in style.

**In 2021, Pramod Bhagat was awarded the prestigious Khel Ratna, the highest award for a sportsperson in the country.**

After that, Pramod's fame and skill just grew with every passing year. Whether it was individual events or doubles or even mixed doubles, everything he touched turned to gold. In no time, Pramod had reached number two in world rankings. More medals and trophies followed, after which he was felicitated by state and central governments. But there was one dream that remained unfulfilled.

Pramod had managed to win every single tournament he had entered in except the Paralympics. He was eagerly awaiting 2020 Tokyo when the pandemic happened. When the Games finally took place in 2021, Pramod found his newest rival. Daniel Bethell was the new Pramod on the bloc, having beaten some high rankers, including Pramod himself, in the past few years. In the semifinal, Bethell defeated another Indian shuttler, Manoj Sarkar, with ease. Manoj had been the only player at the Paralympics so far who had taken a game off Pramod. The scene looked set for a clash for the ages.

And while the scorecard might show that it was a cakewalk for Pramod, it was anything but. Daniel played shots that Pramod was well-versed with, but he still struggled. But in the end, the dream had been realized. He was the greatest para-shuttler that ever existed, having cemented himself as the world number one.

A career with a whopping twenty-six gold medals, a Khel Ratna and a Padma Shri would be an enviable one for any athlete. But Pramod is far from done with his. There are still laurels to go for, and tournaments to win for this champion.

# Know More ...

Racquet sports, whether tennis, badminton or table tennis, constitute the most popular disciplines in the Paralympics, thanks to the speed and reflexes of the athletes. It is also not a surprise to see them therefore compete in the Olympics and other able-bodied events, like five-time Paralympic table tennis champion Natalia Partyka of Poland, who has competed at the Olympics thrice, in 2008, 2012 and 2016.

But when it comes to fast-paced sports, perhaps no record is as astounding as that of Dutch wheelchair tennis legend Esther Vergeer, who retired in 2012 after an unbelievable seven Paralympics golds and a 470 match-winning streak!

INDIA

## Thulasimathi Murugesan

**SU5 BADMINTON**

The two girls beamed at each other as they looked at their medals. 'This means that we are number two in the world!' one of them exclaimed, and they hugged excitedly. The adrenaline from winning the Fazza Dubai Para Badminton International 2023 still hadn't worn off and the shiny gold medals still hung from their necks. The other girl examined the gold and smiled contentedly to herself, murmuring like a mantra, 'Next time, we'll be world number one.'

Her partner giggled at the announcement, "All in good time, Thulasi. Let's just enjoy the moment now. A gold medal doesn't come about every day."

The girl named Thulasimathi agreed, but still reminded herself of her ultimate ambition.

Thulasimathi Murugesan was born in Kancheepuram, Tamil Nadu in 2002 into a family of modest means. The family of four managed to just make ends meet. Right from an early age, Thulasimathi and her sister were encouraged to go out and play all kinds of sports by their father, who was a huge sports buff himself. And while he wanted to play professionally, the family's financial situation meant that the endeavour remained a dream.

Thulasimathi was born with extremely limited movement in her left hand, and often suffered shooting pains in the affected hand. But her father never treated her any different from other kids and insisted on training both his daughters equally in badminton. The sisters would wake up at 4:30am to start their training which continued through the day. It reached a point where Murugesan and his daughters looked like they were enacting a scene from a film – the father ceaselessly training the girls and watching over their progress, and relatives making fun of him for spending so much time with his daughters rather than taking up small jobs to supplement the family income. But Murugesan had a dream, and his daughters were the key to achieving it.

While Thulasimathi learnt and improved her game, she was unable to become a professional sportsperson. The two sisters had entered a few open tournaments with considerable success, but Thulasimathi had not been allowed to compete with other able-bodied peers. Frustrated by this, she vented to her father, who finally had to admit what she had always suspected—she was different. With their insubstantial resources and Murugesan's limited expertise, there was only so far that Thulasimathi could go. But now that the truth was out, she could start looking at the avenues that were open to her.

Thulasimathi started studying to be a veterinarian because the work interested her and was a route out of poverty for her family, but the dream she and her father shared remained intact. Just like in a film, at the right time, she was discovered by the right person. Irfan Khan, a badminton coach at the Gopichand Academy in Hyderabad, saw Thulasimathi play and realized that he had found a diamond. Irfan primarily worked with para-athletes at the Academy, and on his insistence, Thulasimathi left her home for the posh environs of Hyderabad, where she started training to be a professional badminton player.

Alongside a sterling singles career, Thulasimathi also has a formidable doubles career, and has won multiple medals in both women's and mixed formats.

She had to drop a year of her studies, but once there, Thulasimathi didn't look back. She started making headway, and it was not long before everyone at the academy realized what Irfan Khan had earlier. It also helped that in this environment, Thulasimathi had the support and expertise she needed. More than that, she found lifelong friends there, including her doubles partner, Manasi Joshi, who also became a mentor. Being the older of the two, and with considerable educational and work experience, Manasi helped Thulasimathi expand her horizons beyond badminton.

Meanwhile, her badminton skills had reached the level where her coaches thought that she should start competing in international tournaments. In 2023, the chance arrived as Thulasimathi was selected for the Asian Para Games in Hangzhou. She entered the women's singles, the women's doubles with Manasi and mixed doubles with Nitesh Kumar. Thulasimathi made the most of the opportunity—winning three medals, one gold in singles, one silver in doubles with Manasi and one bronze in the mixed doubles with Nitesh Kumar. There was no hint of nerves as she breezed through every match. Her biggest weakness was her backhand, since it required her to move in a way that made her lose her balance due to the lack of mobility in her left hand. But having practiced this at the Academy day in and day out, she was able to overcome this weakness.

The 2023 Games were just a highlight; Thulasimathi kicked it up a notch later in the year. At the Fazza Dubai Para Badminton International, she took another step forward. Along with Manasi, she won the gold, reaching the world number two ranking. Later on, the pair again won the gold at the Canadian Para Badminton International, and en route to it beat the world number one pair and Paralympic champions from Indonesia. At the end of the year, Thulasimathi had amassed an eye-popping ten gold, eight silver and three bronze medals.

At the Paralympics in Paris in 2024, Thulasimathi Murugesan became the first Indian women to win a medal in badminton, clinching a silver in the singles category. By her own high standards, it wasn't the medal she had been dreaming of. But at only twenty-two, there is a truckload of medals waiting for her as she cements her greatness every time she steps on the court.

# Club Throw

Dharambir

# Dharambir Nain

## F51 CLUB THROW

The contest had ended and the results had been declared. The veteran athlete had finished fourth, agonizingly short of a medal. As his young charge and co-competitor came up to him to console him on the missed opportunity, the athlete smiled and slapped his friend on the back. 'That was good, was it not, Dharam?'

The younger athlete was confused but nodded. He had always known his mentor to look at the bright side of everything, so this wasn't out of character for him. They were separated by only four years, but the older athlete had earned the respect and admiration of his competitor, who he also coached. Now the athlete disappeared and the coach emerged. 'You did well too,' he said to Dharambir.

'Amit bhai, I came ninth. I didn't do any—'

The coach interrupted the athlete. 'You think you'll win the gold in your first attempt, huh? Look at where you were two years ago, Dharam. And where you are now.'

As they left the arena, the coach said, 'The medal will come. It will come.'

This was the 2016 Rio Paralympics, where Amit Kumar Saroha, India's medal hope in club throw, missed the podium by a whisker. His young charge was Dharambir Nain, who was competing in his first Paralympics. For someone who had started learning the sport just two years ago, the ninth rank was a great result for Dharambir.

**Club throw is a parasport that tests arm dynamism, much like the hammer throw in the Olympics.**

Club throw is a specialized sport that is played only at the Paralympics. Its Olympic equivalent is the hammer throw, and the rules for both are similar. Instead of a hammer, athletes throw a wooden club with a heavy metallic end. The stance to throw is mostly static, with the club being swung over the head to give it momentum. Prior to Amit and Dharambir taking it up, the sport did not have any recognized facilities in the country, as was the case with other throwing sports like javelin, discus and shot put.

Dharambir Nain was born in 1989 in Badana village, Haryana. Dharambir always had a yearning for the outdoors, and like most youth growing up in farmer families, he helped his parents at the farm. In his free time, he ran about in the fields, swam in the canals and played truant with his friends. After finishing his undergraduate degree, Dharambir joined Maharshi Dayanand University in Rohtak for his master's. During this time, he went on a short trip to a relative's place with his friends. There, while jumping into a canal for a swim, Dharambir ended up seriously injuring his spine. This confined him to a wheelchair for the rest of his life.

As a young person who loved physical activities and who was also dealing with the recent demise of his father, this incident hit Dharambir hard. While undergoing recovery, he often wondered what he was going to do with his life. He had been bedridden for a year when the most unexpected of meetings took place. A friend of Dharambir's knew Amit Kumar Saroha and asked him to visit his friend and help him out. Amit is a stalwart of para athletics, and several Paralympians across disciplines owe their careers to him. When he met Dharambir, Amit said just one thing to his would-be disciple, 'Son, there are only two choices for you. Either you can smile and live a happy life. Or you can stay sad and let it be a burden. Which one will it be?'

Something about Amit's manner of speaking sparked a fire in Dharambir. Knowing his love for sports, Amit introduced Dharambir to discus and club throw, sports that he was able to pick up within a year. Both coach and disciple shared the podium at the 2015 National Para Athletics Championship, and Dharambir made his Paralympics debut the year after. By then, Dharambir was top of the class in domestic tournaments. But an international medal still eluded him. Amit, for his part, was uncompromising during training and supportive during tournaments. 'The medal will come. You just do your best,' was his advice to Dharambir every time.

And it did pay off. In 2018, at the Asian Para Games in Jakarta, Dharambir won his first international medal – a silver. This gave him hope that there would be a change in fortune at the next Paralympics. But it wasn't to be, as Dharambir finished at a frustrating eighth. Even though he and Amit could see a marked improvement in his style and strength, it wasn't translating to medals. But just like Amit had said, all that was needed was patience and game management. 2022 was Dharambir's best year, where he finished with two silver medals, one at the Asian Para Games, where Amit took home the bronze. It seemed like the stage was set for Amit to pass the torch on to Dharambir.

The moment arrived at the Paris Paralympics in 2024. Dharambir was making good throws, but he was also collecting a lot of fouls, which was perhaps because of nerves. Amit, who was also competing in the event, could see that their game plan was coming undone because of that. He started coaching and calming Dharambir during the event, talking to him after every throw, giving him the confidence he needed.

Amit finished tenth in that event. But he had the biggest smile during the podium ceremony. Dharambir, with a throw of 34.92 metres, had broken the Asian record and won the gold. From a measly 13 metres when he picked up the sport, Dharambir stood at the pinnacle of it ten years later. All thanks to his perseverance and the constant support of his coach, confidant and best friend, Amit Saroha.

# High Jump

# Mariyappan Thangavelu

## T42 & T63 HIGH JUMP

As the family stood looking in awe at what was going to be their new home, the matriarch teared up. She had told her son that a paddy field was more than enough for them all. But the field was just the first surprise. This was much bigger than any of them had imagined.

Flanked by her children, the mother walked inside. She looked at the freshly painted walls and the wide spaces, knowing that nothing would be the same for them ever again. But then she had had this realization ever since she saw her son in the Paralympics final. Everything since then had been a blur, but this moment, with them standing in silence and just basking in the glory of their turn of fortune, brought everything home. She kissed her son on the forehead, believing herself to be the luckiest woman in the world.

But luck took its time to reach their lives. Mariyappan Thangavelu was born in 1995 in Salem, Tamil Nadu. With an elder sister and two younger brothers, responsibility fell on him at a very early age, especially as his mother, a vegetable vendor, was struggling to provide for her children.

Despite the hardships, Mariyappan's mother wanted to make sure that her children were educated. To her delight, her eldest son was fond of studying. She saw his drive and interest as the key to a better life. However, an accident put a pause on their lives. In 2000, while Mariyappan was walking to school, a drunk driver ran over his right knee, which resulted in the stunted development of his right leg. The family came under severe financial strain due to Mariyappan's treatment and recuperation, but their mother never let them feel so, instead forgoing her own meals and working extra hours to pay the bills.

It was this love and care that allowed Mariyappan to be involved in sports alongside his studies. He enjoyed playing volleyball and had a great reach for someone so young and short. His physical education teacher saw his standing jump and thought that the young boy would be suited to high jump. This suggestion and the coaching that followed would forever change the course of Mariyappan's life.

As he got better and better at high jump, his coach and teacher decided to enter him in an open athletics tournament. At the age of fourteen, Mariyappan, competing among students who had more experience and exposure than him, showed nerves of steel. He finished the competition in second place, showing what he was capable of. With the encouragement of his classmates and his teachers, he decided to compete professionally as a para athlete. This was a huge change for a boy who had vowed to complete his studies and concentrate on getting a good job. As was the case then, sports outside cricket and hockey did not get much funding, and for a family that needed money desperately, athletics wasn't a wise choice of vocation. But Mariyappan's mother supported him wholeheartedly. When he was away for training, his siblings pitched in to make up for his absence.

As he started participating in more and more tournaments at the state and national level, people started noticing Mariyappan and marking him as one to look out for. At the National Para Athletics Championships in 2013, Mariyappan was noticed by national level coach Satyanarayana, who, after watching him perform a few times, decided to take him to Bengaluru for further training. Satyanarayana, who had exclusively worked with para athletes, was surprised at how refined and superior Mariyappan's technique was. It was only a matter of time before the boy would be winning medals, he thought.

And the coach was proven right. Soon after he was taken in as a student in 2015, Mariyappan's first international tournament arrived. This was the International Para Championships Grand Prix, held in Tunisia in March 2016. With a jump of 1.78 metres, his personal best, Mariyappan qualified for the 2016 Paralympics in Rio.

At the Paralympics later that year, all eyes were on Mariyappan. People had been doubting him for far too long. Now there was anticipation and hope that maybe, just maybe, this young athlete would get India its first medal in high jump.

The hope was not misplaced at all. Mariyappan bettered his previous best, jumping a mammoth 1.89 metres on his way to a historic gold. Back then, it made him the third Indian to win a gold at the Paralympics. His feat won him the admiration of the entire nation as well as accolades like the Padma Shri

In recognition of his sporting excellence, Mariyappan has been conferred the Arjuna Award (2017), the Padma Shri (2017) and the Khel Ratna (2020).

and the Arjuna Award. After this major victory, Mariyappan decided to give back to those who had supported him in his journey. He purchased a paddy field for his mother, so that she did not have to work anymore, in addition to a comfortable house.

For his part, Mariyappan is still going strong in his field, inspiring others and still winning medals, despite changing his category from T42 to T63. The gold might not have come his way again since then, but there is hope that it will in the future.

# Know More ...

Para athletics is among the most competitive sports in the world, across abilities and disciplines. Since its inception in the inaugural Paralympics, there have been 109 countries that have won at least one medal in para athletics, the most for any sport. This diversity of winners makes para athletics one of the most exciting sports to watch, and one of the likeliest places to watch an underdog win. From 31 athletes participating in 25 medal events in 1960, there were 1,069 para athletes competing in 164 medal events in 2024. Talk about a competitive field!

# Praveen Kumar

## T44 HIGH JUMP

Dr Satyapal Singh looked sceptically at the young boy in front of him. One of the main things about high jump is height, as it gives an athlete a considerable advantage while jumping. The child in front of him just about reached five and a half feet. He didn't have the heart to tell this young athlete that his height was a considerable disadvantage—it is difficult when you have someone so passionate standing in front of you. So the coach asked the boy to try. If he couldn't do it, then Satyapal wouldn't have to say anything. The young dreamer would understand.

The athlete took his run up and jumped. Not only did he easily clear it, but he did it so cleanly that it left Satyapal astounded. The boy had perhaps the mightiest right leg he had seen. And so, instead of dissuading a young soul from aiming for the stars, Satyapal became his biggest believer, taking on the onus of training the young Praveen Kumar.

Born in 2003, Praveen hailed from a small village near Jewar in Gautam Buddh Nagar, Uttar Pradesh. Belonging to a poor farming family, he was born with a congenital disorder that hindered the development of his left leg. Despite these challenges, he was never treated differently, and often enjoyed playing with his friends and going to school.

In some ways, Praveen's story is similar to Mariyappan Thangavelu's. While at school, Praveen enjoyed playing volleyball, and much like Mariyappan, he also had a short stature. But his height was never an impediment, as Praveen's right leg muscles were so developed that he had immense reach and was often the star player on his team. His friends often told him to switch to athletics, but Praveen initially ignored it. He knew that he would be turned away from able-bodied competitions owing to his left leg. But owing to the continuing pressure from his schoolmates, Praveen decided to look it up online.

Praveen discovered the world of Paralympics on the internet, and he also found out about the legend of Mariyappan Thangavelu, who had just won the gold at Rio. Praveen decided that at the next Paralympics, he would be the one on the top step. And this wasn't an empty promise. Praveen started working on his technique from the very next day, and found out about the district and state-level tournaments he could participate in.

When it came to junior-level events, it was hard not to notice Praveen. He was head and shoulders above the rest, and he jumped so high that it often left people shocked at his ability to do so. Praveen even decided to try his luck at an open event, where he could participate against the so-called 'able-bodied' young athletes. While he did not win the event, Praveen found something even more important.

At the event, he was introduced to Ashok Saini, a former gymnastics coach who was working in Haryana's Sports and Youth Affairs department. Saini was impressed with Praveen's performance and gave him the contact of Dr Satyapal Singh for further guidance. Praveen contacted Satyapal, and after a trial that blew the coach away, he was accepted as his charge. They were a perfect fit–like Praveen, Satyapal Singh also wanted to win the gold in Tokyo.

In 2018, Praveen started training with his coach, and in less than a year, he was sent off to his first major international tournament, the World Para Athletics Junior Championships. There, he won a silver, and followed it up with a fourth-place finish at the Senior Championships. Additionally, he won his very first gold at the Fazza International Championships in Dubai. Praveen soon started getting outside financial support in the form of sponsorships.

It looked like the Paralympic gold was within reach going into 2020, but it wasn't to be. The pandemic raged on from March, pressing pause on all sporting events and preventing Praveen from training for long periods. By the time the lockdown ended, Praveen had contracted COVID-19 and had to be isolated for that. It was feared that he wouldn't be able to make it to Tokyo, but Praveen got better and managed to make the flight.

**At the age of just twenty one, Praveen has managed to amass a staggering collection of medals and has broken the Asian record on multiple occasions.**

It was Praveen's first Paralympics. He went in with the aim of competing well so that he remained motivated to try again. He ended up breaking the Asian record and won a silver. While his last attempt, which could have easily won him the gold, did not go according to plan, it was a promising showing from the athlete, who became India's youngest Paralympics medallist at the age of seventeen.

'Don't worry, beta. Next time we'll get the gold and the record too,' his coach Satyapal Singh maintained, and Praveen believed it. He knew that if he had trained and not caught COVID-19, that gold would have been his. Returning home to fanfare and celebrations, Praveen threw himself into preparing and getting better with even more energy. But he did not neglect his education, enrolling for a bachelor's degree at Motilal Nehru College at Delhi University.

On the turf, Praveen continued amassing medals, winning the gold in the 2022 Asian Para Games in Hangzhou, adding to India's already humongous tally at the event. He again broke the Asian record on the way to a bronze at the World Para Athletics Championships in the same year. But it was a Paralympic gold that was on his mind. He prayed there wouldn't be any obstacles this time.

As 2024 rolled around, Praveen felt it to be the culmination of everything he had been doing over the past three years. The event in Paris was unlike anything in Tokyo. While in 2021, Praveen had often made mistakes while landing and cleared his jumps after multiple attempts, now he was at the peak of his game. Every single attempt that he went for, from 1.89 metres to 2.08 metres, was perfect. Praveen Kumar again broke the Asian record as he took home the gold and wrote his name in history.

At just twenty-one years of age, more medals and the world record still beckon to Praveen.

# Javelin Throw

0562

## Devendra Jhajharia

**F46 JAVELIN**

While Neeraj Chopra was on his way to becoming a household name after winning the gold at the 2020 Tokyo Olympics in the javelin throw, there was another son of the soil who was dejected at landing a silver. His competitors congratulated him, and the Indian contingent was cheering with all its might on winning another medal. But his coach knew how his favourite athlete was feeling.

He patted the javelin thrower's shoulder, and they hugged. 'This makes you the most decorated athlete from India,' he said consolingly.

The athlete sighed and smiled weakly, 'A third gold would have been better.'

Devendra Jhajharia was born in 1981 in the town of Churu in Rajasthan. While Churu is known as the gateway to the Thar desert, thanks to its proximity to the shifting dunes of the desert, to Devendra, it was his ultimate playground. He would run about with his friends, climbing trees and ancient monuments with an adroitness that was surprising even to his peers. From an early age, his family felt Devendra was more suited to a life of adventure and games and expected him to join the armed forces.

However, destiny finds ways of upending even the most predictable of lives. At the age of eight, while climbing a tree with his friends, Devendra inadvertently touched a live electric wire. He was rushed to the hospital, where the doctors were able to save his life. However, they could not save his left hand, which had to be amputated.

But this setback did not deter Devendra from continuing to play games. Slowly but not surprisingly, Devendra became one of the star athletes of his school. There wasn't a sports day that went by without him winning a medal in some discipline.

At one school event in 1997, his performances caught the eye of legendary para-sports coach and future Dronacharya awardee R.D. Singh, who took him under his wing and started training Devendra for track and field. Of all the disciplines, it was javelin throw that Devendra took to. Having done most tasks with just his right hand for nearly ten years, it was perhaps the strongest part of his body, and when the javelin left his hand, there was just awe among the onlookers. R.D. Singh had discovered a gem that seemed to shine already!

After winning several accolades internationally, Devendra managed to qualify for the Paralympics in 2004. The news was still awash with then Capt. Rajyavardhan Rathore's exploits in Athens, having won India's first individual silver. As Indian athletes rarely scored individual medals, there were low expectations from the country's contingent at the Paralympics as well, which was reflected in a mere twelve participants in the Games. But Devendra was all set to change this.

In his six attempts, Devendra broke the world record by some distance, landing the javelin at 62.15 meters, as opposed to the previous one which stood at 59.77 meters. The effort landed him the gold medal and legendary status. People were amazed as to how an Indian athlete could so easily break the world record, especially someone they had not heard of before. For his efforts, Devendra was felicitated with the Arjuna Award, among other national accolades.

Devendra Jhajharia can be credited with kickstarting India's Paralympic revolution all the way back in 2004, when he broke the world record and won the gold.

But instead of resting on his laurels, Devendra was hungry for more. Even though he was married now and had secured a lucrative job with the Indian Railways, the adventure seeker and outdoor lover in him refused to go away. After a short sabbatical, Devendra was back to winning consecutive medals at the World Para Athletics Championships from 2013 to 2015. In 2016, he won the gold at the IPC Athletics Asia-Oceania Championships in Dubai. This return to form happened at just the right time. Devendra had qualified for the Rio Paralympics and was raring to go. It had been twelve years since his gold. Would he win it again?

Devendra not only won the gold by some margin, but also broke the world record again, this time landing the javelin at a stunning 63.97 meters. Not just India, but the world was astounded at the feat, and decided to raise their hands in acknowledgement of an athlete who refused to see any limit, and who was always hungry for more. The government conferred the Khel Ratna on Devendra Jhajharia.

A few years later, at the 2020 Tokyo Paralympics, as he stood at the podium receiving his silver medal, Devendra was not as dejected as he had initially been. Standing next to him was his compatriot Sundar Singh Gurjar, who had won the bronze. From being the only medal winner, to being one among many, perhaps this was part of Devendra's legacy too. He had brought the country to the forefront at the Paralympics.

# Know More ...

Alongside Boccia, Goalball is the only other sport at the Paralympics that does not have an Olympic equivalent.

Primarily designed for visually impaired athletes, Goalball consists of teams of three, where the aim is to throw (not kick) the ball into the opponent's goal, while the opponent attempts to block it. To aid the players, the ball has bells on the inside so that athletes can hear and follow it, testing their ear-hand coordination. Whoever has more goals in two halves of twelve minutes each wins!

SUMIT

## Sumit Antil

**F64 JAVELIN**

As the storied career of Devendra Jhajharia came to a close with a silver at the 2020 Paralympics, there was another star who had decided to step into his shoes and carry the flame for Indian javelin throwers. No, we aren't talking of Neeraj Chopra, but a contemporary of his who always ends up winning medals and breaking records whenever he steps onto the field. This is Sumit Antil, the current toast of the town and the new legend in the world of javelin.

Sumit was born in 1998 in Sonipat, Haryana. Growing up in rural Haryana and belonging to the Jat community, he was exposed to wrestling from childhood and became interested in the sport. Sumit's father was employed with the Indian Air Force. When Sumit was just six years old, his father decided that he would be a wrestler. Unexpectedly, his father passed away soon after, and Sumit's resolve became even stronger. He would wrestle, and he would join the army. And it seemed like a forgone conclusion, as Sumit was extremely athletic and passionate about sports.

But life had other plans. In 2015, while riding a motorcycle on his way back from his tuition classes, Sumit met with an accident when a speeding truck hit him. He was rushed to the hospital, where his left leg had to be amputated. He recovered soon after, but his dream was lost. Sumit couldn't join the army now, and his wrestling days were perhaps behind him too. Sumit decided to concentrate on his studies.

He did well academically, and managed to secure admission to the BCom programme of Ramjas College, Delhi University. At college, Sumit met Rajkumar, a fellow student and a para-athlete. Rajkumar, seeing that Sumit was of a similar athletic build, introduced his friend to para athletics, and recommended that he try it out since he had both the strength and the talent. As someone who had always loved sports, Sumit was enthusiastic about the idea. He started his formal training in 2017 and soon picked javelin as his favoured discipline.

Among his first major events was the 2019 World Para Athletics Grand Prix in Grosseto, Italy. Sumit participated in the combined event, which pooled in all the para-athletes irrespective of their category into one event. He broke the world record in the F64 category and landed the silver in the event. In November of the same year, Sumit participated in the World Para Athletics Championships in Dubai, where he won a second silver, as he again broke the world record for his category.

But before the Paralympics could take place, the COVID-19 pandemic took hold all over the world and delayed events by almost a year. This gap allowed Sumit to work even harder on his skills and technique as he wanted to leave no stone unturned in his bid for gold.

After almost a year's delay, the Tokyo Paralympics finally took place. And Sumit was prepared and ready to take on whatever came his way. On 30 August 2021, Sumit did what he had done two years ago—he broke the world record again. This time, however, he won the gold. With a monumental throw of 68.55 metres, Sumit broke the world record in three successive throws, each better than the last, leaving the entire world in awe. If that wasn't enough, in the same year, Sumit broke the world record yet again at the Indian Open National Para Athletics Championships, bettering his previous mark to a new milestone of 68.62 metres.

Now there was no stopping Sumit. After years of knockbacks and recovery and lingering pain, this achievement was a testament to his resilience, and his refusal to give up. It was this will power that contributed to his meteoric rise and fed his constant hunger for more medals and records.

The year after the Tokyo Paralympics, Sumit was at it again. At the 2022 Hangzhou Asian Para Games, he broke the world record one more time as he won the gold yet again. This is an all-category record that is yet to be broken and stands at an eye-popping 73.29 metres. It was starting to get absurd now, to the point where competitors knew that they were competing for silver the moment Sumit set foot in the arena. He followed this up with successive gold medals at the World Para Championships in Paris and Kobe in 2023 and 2024.

The Paris Paralympics rolled around. This time, there was no question of who would be get the gold. Sumit Antil was participating, so the only thing that had to be seen was whether he would break his incredible record from two years ago or not.

Sumit won the gold, as was expected. He also ended up breaking the Paralympic record twice during his performance. But he couldn't better his own throw, which has become the stuff of legends. That isn't to say, however, that he won't break this record. After all, the man is still in his twenties. There are plenty of championships, grand prix and Paralympics remaining to be conquered. The legend of Sumit Antil is still going strong.

Sumit has held the World Record for para-javelin an astonishing six times! He currently holds both the World Record (73.29m) and the Paralympic Record (70.59m).

# Know More ...

Several Paralympic events have 'assistants' or 'guides' to help the players compete to the best of their abilities. In visually impaired running disciplines, there is a 'guide runner' who is lightly tethered to the athlete and helps them maintain direction. Similarly, acoustic devices, or 'callers', are present in throwing or jumping disciplines to indicate the take-off point or the limits of the throwing area. Even the wheelchairs used in football, basketball, rugby and racing are specialized to each discipline, with some prioritizing aerodynamics, while others look to maximize the area of contact.

# Navdeep Singh

## F41 JAVELIN

Among the several stories of inspiration that grabbed the public imagination following the Paris Paralympics, there's one athlete who has found himself slowly turning into a pop-culture icon. And no doubt it is a mixture of his feisty and often witty responses that make people gravitate towards him. As he carves a niche for himself, it hasn't been the easiest of journeys for Navdeep Singh.

The mercurial athlete was born in 2000 in Panipat, to a farming family. Navdeep's father, Dalbir Singh, was a national-level wrestler and was very well respected in his village. Navdeep was born prematurely, which caused a few health issues at the beginning of his life, but he fought those off admirably. However, when he was two, the doctor diagnosed him with dwarfism, which led him to have a shorter stature than most of his peers.

His family, including his elder brother, were very protective of Navdeep and never denied him anything. His father encouraged his son to pursue sports, and Navdeep was more than happy to, as he had always wanted to be a wrestler like him. He therefore started training for it.

However, the situation outside his home was a total contrast. Due to his shorter stature, Navdeep became the butt of insults and jokes, from classmates, neighbours and even random strangers. When it started, Navdeep would run home, shut himself up in his room and not emerge for hours on end. But as he processed the treatment meted out to him, his young mind also developed its own feistiness. Navdeep's mental fortitude manifested through sometimes confrontational, but mostly witty and humorous barbs, which would at most times shut his bullies up.

As he trained and progressed as a wrestler, Navdeep was also aware of the financial struggle that most athletes go through. He therefore did not neglect his studies. After his national-level career, Dalbir Singh had to start dairy farming like the rest of his family, and while the respect he held in the village eventually got him the position of Gram Sachiv, he did not want his son to remain limited to Panipat. Navdeep therefore studied with the intent of getting into a prestigious college and having a fulfilling career.

At the age of sixteen, a crucial development occurred in Navdeep's life that altered his sporting career. In 2016, Navdeep saw a young Neeraj Chopra break the junior world javelin record at the World U20 Championships and was greatly inspired. This was still four years before Neeraj became a household name, but Navdeep had found his calling and his hero. He started preparing to become a javelin athlete in earnest, and while he was not following in his father's footsteps, his family was only too happy for him to start training for the field event.

The following year, Navdeep made his own debut at the Asian Youth Para Games. And like his new idol, he also came away with the gold from his very first international event. He looked set to become the new star of the arena with his passionate approach and intense training. But while the start to his career was explosive, things soon started to taper off, and Navdeep struggled with several issues.

Back then, he lived with fellow Paralympian Sumit Antil, spending most of his time at the SAI training facilities in Gandhinagar and Bengaluru. Homesickness, as well as what some of his critics called his 'temperamental approach', along with recurrent health issues contributed to his struggle, as Navdeep faced a small drought of medals. While he managed to qualify for the 2020 Paralympics, he did not win a medal, finishing fourth. While it was an admirable finish, it was nowhere near the lofty goals Navdeep had set for himself, and he felt dejected.

In 2021, at the World Para Grand Prix in Dubai, there was hope of a return to form as Navdeep captured the gold, but his struggles still continued. With the brilliantly strong contingent of Indian javelin throwers continuing to excel internationally, critics wrote off Navdeep, claiming that he tended to do well in national competitions, but didn't seem to have the gumption for international events.

But Navdeep proved them wrong! After a change in diet and training programme, Navdeep emerged a new athlete, stronger and fitter, but still holding on to his feisty demeanour and approach. His father, who had always been his biggest supporter and idol, passed away early in 2024, which hit him hard. But Navdeep was made of sterner stuff, and even when grieving, he did not let up on his training.

He won the bronze at the World Para Athletics Championships in Kobe a few months later with a personal best, which qualified him for the 2024 Paralympics. He had his opportunity to atone for what he thought had been his fault the last time, and to pay tribute to his father.

In Paris, as Navdeep lined up to take his first attempt, he was tense. It wasn't a clean attempt, and Navdeep was sorely disappointed with the result. As he walked back, his coach playfully reprimanded him, but Navdeep, usually ready with a witty comeback, did not even crack a smile. He was already in his zone now.

> Navdeep emulated his hero Neeraj Chopra's 2016 World U20 Championship gold with a gold in the 2017 Asian Youth Para Games on his debut.

The second throw was much better and placed him with the upper level of the competitors. The third throw, which went viral, showed all the energy, anger and disappointment that Navdeep had experienced so far condense into one moment. As soon as the javelin left his hand, he knew that this was the throw he had been waiting for. It broke the Paralympic record and pushed him right up to first place.

On the fifth attempt, however, the drama continued, as Iran's Sadegh Beit Sayah outperformed him to clinch the gold. That was, until he was disqualified on technical grounds. The new record and the gold went to Navdeep, who looked up to the sky in gratitude. The demons of the past had been exorcised, and all that was left was the future, smiling at him with more medals in store.

# *Judo*

## Kapil Parmar

### J1 JUDO

As the struggle ensued, spectators could sense the exhaustion of the two athletes. There had been several bouts before this, and this final match for a medal appeared to be an even contest. Then, as if to set the record straight, one of the athletes was thrown on to the mat, resulting in an ippon, the highest score possible in judo. The fall was met with a loud cheer from the Indian contingent, all of whom rose up to applaud a dominant display. The judoka was delighted and jumped up in joy.

Later, as he felt the medal in his hands, Kapil Parmar had only one thing to say to his coach: 'Sir, I'll get a gold at Los Angeles. Promise.'

Kapil Parmar was born in 2000 in Sehore, a town near Bhopal in Madhya Pradesh. His father, a taxi driver, and mother, a farm labourer, did their best to provide for their children and take care of their every need. Since Kapil was also the youngest among four brothers and sisters, he was a bit more indulged than the rest.

Kapil loved wrestling with his elder brother and was fond of running about and exploring his village while helping his parents. One day, he was sent to fetch water from the pump. Unbeknownst to him, some of the water had leaked out around the pump, and as soon as Kapil touched it, he felt an extremely strong electric shock. A villager found an unconscious Kapil by the pump shortly after. He was rushed to the hospital, where he would spend the next six months in a coma. Throughout this time, his family never lost hope, trying their best to finance his care and recovery. When Kapil emerged from the coma, his body had considerably shrunk and atrophied. The doctors advised Kapil to gain weight once discharged, in order to prevent any complications for his still growing body.

The hospital stay was also a considerable financial hit on the family. To help pay for his recovery, Kapil helped his siblings run a tea stall, which managed to ease some of the financial burden. In the meanwhile, Kapil had managed to find a way to develop his physical strength that would change his life in ways he had never imagined.

Having loved wrestling, Kapil decided to get into judo. He had coaches and teachers around him who were more than happy to show him the ropes and help him strengthen. Kapil felt the strength return to his body slowly. His elder brother was also a judo enthusiast, so they would often spar and train with each other.

Two years after the accident, Kapil's eyesight started deteriorating. The doctors couldn't do much about it, indicating that this was a fallout from the electrocution. He was given spectacles with extremely high power, but even those failed after a few months. Kapil was left with minimal vision, and it was tough to figure out the way forward.

In para judo, the contest always starts with both the competitors having a loose grip on each other's judo suits, which is called 'Kumikata'.

But if there was anything Kapil could count on, it was his family's support and love. His brother introduced him to para judo and Paralympics, which gave Kapil the hope that he could still play the sport that had quickly become his favourite. He continued to train and practice with his brother in their village. Some villagers admired Kapil's resolve, while others taunted him about his vision, laughing at his desire to be a judoka. For his part, Kapil took the jeers as motivation to do better.

At the age of seventeen, Kapil had learnt all he could from his brother, but he was hungry for more. He joined the Indian Blind and Para Judo Academy in Lucknow, where his training and expertise were taken to the next level. He met his coach Munawar Anzar Ali Siddiqui there, and the two built a formidable partnership. As Kapil's coach, Munawar wanted to give his athlete plenty of time to rest and enjoy life, so as to be able to undertake intense training before the tournaments.

After winning several junior and national level tournaments, in 2019, Kapil participated in his first international event, the Commonwealth Judo Championships in Birmingham. This was the first time he was in an unfamiliar location, and his coach would be paramount in helping him win. One of the cornerstones of para judo is the communication between the coach and the athlete. With limited vision, the coach's verbal instructions and information become even more important, and in a way, Munawar Anzar was Kapil's eyes. The two found their rhythm through the bouts, and Kapil ended up winning the gold.

The transformation around Kapil was sudden. The villagers who had been taunting him turned into his biggest supporters, regaling everyone with tales of the brave judoka from Sehore. While his brother Lalit and the income from their shop had helped finance Kapil's domestic tournaments as well as this one, sponsors were now lining up to offer support. His father no longer had to work as a taxi driver, and his mother gave up her part-time job as a farm labourer.

By the time the Paralympics rolled around in 2024, Kapil had won a bevy of medals and was the world number one. A lapse in concentration led the twenty-four-year-old to lose his semifinal bout, but he dominated his bronze medal opponent with a magnificent ippon, winning 10-0.

The dream for the Paralympic gold still remains, and there is little doubt that Kapil will win it in the coming years.

# *Shooting*

# Avani Lekhara

## SH1 10 M AIR RIFLE

When it comes to sports that require aim, it has been found that participants often look for the perfect score rather than the medal. That was the reason behind Harvinder Singh's brilliance at archery, as well as Sumit Antil's javelin genius. It is also the case with Avani Lekhara, who ranks among India's greatest sportswomen.

At the Tokyo Paralympics in 2021, Avani felt a bit listless after the final round as everyone around her celebrated. She had scored an incredible 9.9. Shooters are scored on the basis of their accuracy, and the shooting target is made up of ten concentric circles, with the outermost circle giving a score of 1, and the innermost a score of 10. In latter stages of the competition, each circle is divided into a further ten zones, with a decimal point awarded for how close to the bullseye is the shot. A 9.9 meant that Avani's score was the highest possible in the penultimate circle of the target, which had landed her a historic gold. But that didn't matter to her. She was looking for a 10.9.

Avani Lekhara was born in November 2001 in Jaipur in a middle-class family. Both her parents worked as tax officials and Avani grew up in a happy home. Once she started schooling, everyone, from her teachers to her classmates, noted her brilliance in studies. She enjoyed studying, and could not see herself being away from her books for too long.

In 2012, however, things changed drastically. Avani was involved in a very serious car accident, which left her paraplegic and wheelchair bound. This was a tremendous setback, but Avani's parents never let her feel like there was anything missing, providing her with every aid to make her life and movement easier. Her father, understanding that the lack of physical activity might adversely affect Avani's health, introduced her to sports.

Avani had always been more interested in studies with minimal inclination towards sports. But on her father's insistence, she picked up archery. She found the sport challenging but enjoyable. Spending time at the archery range made Avani feel better about herself.

The big change arrived when Avani read Abhinav Bindra's biography. Having seen interviews and news of India's then only individual gold medallist, Avani looked up to Bindra. Inspired by his journey, she picked up the rifle and decided to follow in Bindra's footsteps.

The decision was proven right in a very short time. Avani was a natural when it came to shooting, and her obsession with precision worked in her favour. At the state level championships in 2015–Avani's very first competition–she won the gold, obliterating the rest of the field.

The two years that followed were filled with lots of training and small competitions and tournaments to ready Avani for the big league. In 2017, the opportunity came at the Al Ain World Shooting Para Sport World Cup, where Avani snagged a silver, and then a bronze at the Bangkok World Shooting Para Sport World Cup later in the year. Avani was happier with her performance than with the medals. This helped lay the groundwork for the ultimate aim that she harboured.

In 2018, after a year's experience in the international circuit, Avani emerged as a revelation in the shooting world. At the World Shooting Para Sport World Cup, Avani won three golds in three different disciplines, namely 50 m three position (which uses all stances of standing, kneeling and prone), prone and her default 10 m. Her winning streak continued with several national and international medals in 2019, but she narrowly missed one at the World Shooting Para Sport Championships in Sydney. But what gave Avani and her coaches some satisfaction was that she had improved greatly since the last edition of the Championships in 2018 in South Korea, where she had struggled to qualify.

For her legendary exploits in para shooting, Avani was conferred the Khel Ratna in 2021 and the Padma Shri in 2022.

When the 2020 Tokyo Paralympics arrived, Avani was more than ready. Her coaches and family had helped her train extensively for an extra year due to the lockdown, and she was in peak form going into the tournament.

But this was the Paralympics, and an Indian woman was yet to win a gold in any discipline. And this is where Avani entered the record books.

Spectators were in awe at the score of 249.6 (the cumulative total of all her attempts), which set a new Paralympic record along with equalling the world record as Avani became the first Indian woman to win a gold medal in the 10 m air rifle. As if that wasn't enough, Avani won the bronze in the 50 m rifle event. Thus, at just eighteen years of age, Avani became a star and the government showered her with accolades. She remained committed to her sport and stayed humble in the face of fame and praise.

Following this, it was like the floodgates for medals opened up. At the 2022 World Shooting Para Sports World Cup in Châteauroux in France, Avani completely wiped the floor with the competition on her way to two golds, qualifying for the 2024 Paralympics with ease. But what gave her joy was the fact that she had broken her own world record, scoring a 250.6. This also helped her clinch the world number one spot.

While for a lot of people it might have been a forgone conclusion that Avani would take another gold in 2024, things weren't so easy. Very few paralympians had won back-to-back golds at the highest level. Moreover, Avani had just recovered from a gall bladder surgery, which had thrown her preparation off schedule. And emerging compatriot Mona Agarwal was in good form, having beaten Avani at the National Championships earlier in the year.

Despite the hardships, Avani broke the Paralympic record that she had set the last time, scoring a 249.7 as she bagged the gold, closely beating her competitors. She became the first Indian to win back-to-back gold medals, a feat that was later matched by Sumit Antil at the same Paralympics.

At just twenty-three, the world is Avani's oyster and more medals await her at championships in the future.

# Know More ...

While the Summer Paralympic Games usually take all the eyeballs across the world, there is also a Winter edition that has gained popularity. The Winter Paralympic Games were first held in 1976 in Sweden and since then, have been held in tandem with the Summer Paralympic Games. Featuring six sporting disciplines, the scope of the Winter Paralympics is much smaller than that of its Summer sibling, but it features some of the most adrenalin-pumping disciplines like para snowboarding, para ice hockey and para cross country skiing.

# Mona Agarwal

## SH1 10 M AIR RIFLE

While the world was hailing the brilliance of Avani Lekhara at the 2024 Paris Paralympics, there was another Jaipur resident on that podium who held her head up high and revelled in the glory. As she looked around her with a wide smile, a member of the team ran up to her with a mobile phone. Seeing her two kids over a video call made her tear up. They repeated what they had been saying for quite some time: 'Come home, mummy. Now you can put the GPS on the phone and get here!' They smiled mischievously, which made her laugh. 'On my way, kids. I'm also bringing lots of gifts for both of you.'

Mona Agarwal's route to the top could not have been more different from other athletes. In fact, it was nearly the opposite of her fellow athlete from Jaipur and rival, Avani Lekhara. Mona was born in 1987 in Sikar, Rajasthan. Growing up in a highly conservative society, especially as the third daughter in the family, life was always going to be a challenge for Mona.

The situation worsened when at the tender age of nine months, Mona contracted polio, which significantly impaired her legs. While friends and relatives often berated and insulted her, Mona had one ally who stood by her. Mona's grandmother, Geeta Devi, was a feisty woman, and often came to her granddaughter's defence in front of others. She made it a point to remind Mona that there was nothing she couldn't achieve, giving her the self-belief that with hard work, her handicap could never be an obstacle for her.

After her schooling was cut short due to financial constraints as well as the fact that she was a girl, Mona chose to focus on sports. She was an athletic person, and often played different sports. But that was rather unpalatable to her family and the village. They gave her an ultimatum to put a stop to these activities. Taking inspiration from her grandmother, Mona decided to do the unthinkable. She left home.

From Sikar, Mona moved to Jaipur, where she started competing as a para athlete. This was the early 2010s, and visibility for para athletes, let alone financial support for them, was non-existent. Mona competed across categories and disciplines, from shot put to javelin to weightlifting, winning medals at the state level in almost all categories. She was also an ardent fan of volleyball, a sport that she loved to watch and play. Realizing that there was no para volleyball team in the country, Mona took it upon herself to travel across the nation, drumming up support for the sport and trying to recruit new players into her fledgling team.

Around this time, Mona also got married to Ravindra Chaudhary, a wheelchair basketball player from Jaipur. This gave Mona a support system as her husband and her in-laws both supported her sporting journey as well as her other initiatives. Towards the end of the decade, Mona also became a mother. However, the athlete, who had always been in tune with her body, found that she couldn't keep up with athletics anymore. The strict diet and the jerky movements that the disciplines required were having an adverse effect on her body. Mona was heartbroken at the thought of giving up sports.

Unwilling to give up on her sporting dream, Mona decided to look up sports that were more suited to her abilities and did not require actions that could endanger her health. She soon discovered shooting, but shooting is an expensive sport and requires costly rifles and other equipment. Nevertheless, Mona decided to persevere. Her first visit was to the Eklavya Sports Shooting Academy, where she met coach Yogesh Shekhawat, who was impressed by her passion and resolve. He decided to waive her fees, and together, the two set about finding equipment and arms for Mona to start training.

A seasoned athlete of various sports, Mona made her debut in para shooting in 2023 at the Para Shooting World Cup, where she ended up winning the bronze medal.

This was all shortly after the 2020 Paralympics. With sponsorships, as well as her own savings, Mona managed to purchase a rifle (which usually costs close to ₹25 lakh) as well as other necessary equipment. And thus started her training.

Having powerlifted and competed in athletics before, Mona found it easy to hold her rifle. This core strength helped her hold herself steady while aiming and shooting. After competing in a few domestic tournaments where she completely outplayed her competition, Mona was ready for the big league.

Her first international tournament was the Para Shooting World Cup in Osijek, Croatia in July 2023. Mona was nervous, but she knew that the purpose of this tournament was to train her for the bigger occasions. She won the bronze in the 10 m air rifle team classification, in her international debut. She was elated with the result, and the dream of participating in the Paralympics, even if they were just a year away, seemed real to her.

Mona had competed in three international tournaments by the time 2024 arrived. But unfortunately, around this time, her husband met with a grave accident. She was prepared to give up sports to look after him, but her in-laws asked her to concentrate on her tournaments while they took care of her husband and the children. Armed with this support, Mona got ready for the very first Para Shooting World Cup being held in India.

At the Karni Singh Shooting Range in New Delhi, Mona defied the odds to clinch the gold in the 10 m air rifle and qualified for the Paralympics. And who was the bronze medal winner? None other than defending Paralympics champion Avani Lekhara, who had been bested by her compatriot. The positions might have been reversed at the Paralympics, but Mona Agarwal had finally arrived, proving that it is never too late to find your true calling.

## Know More ...

Several athletes, as already mentioned, have competed in both the Olympics and the Paralympics. Sometimes, the Paralympic records even break existing Olympic ones. For example, Hungarian fencer Pal Szekeres won the bronze in the 1988 Seoul Olympics, and after overcoming adversity in the form of a bus accident in 1991, won the fencing gold in the 1992 Paralympics in Barcelona.

But here's a stat that will truly make you wonder: The top-four finishers of the 1500m race in the T13 category at the 2016 Rio Paralympics clocked faster times than their 'able-bodied' counterparts in the same edition of the Olympics!

## Rubina Francis

### SH1 10 M AIR PISTOL

The event was over and the pistols had fallen silent, all that could be heard was the applause and cheers of the medallists. As the rounds of congratulations and countless hugs continued, one shooter sat disconsolate. It was her first time at the Paralympics, but she had expected to win a medal. From the highest of highs only a few months ago, this felt like the lowest she could go.

Her coach, who had been by her side the entire time, squeezed her shoulder. 'Very well, done, Rubina! Seventh rank! This is the highest any Indian woman has ever finished here.' Upon seeing his charge's expression, he said, 'This is just your first Paralympics, child. You have many more to go and many more medals to win.'

It was difficult for the young athlete to think about anything other than this missed opportunity, but she trusted her coach's words.

Rubina Francis was born in 1999 to a working-class family in Jabalpur, Madhya Pradesh. Her father worked as a mechanic, while her mother was a nurse. Although they faced financial difficulties, Rubina's parents earned enough to make ends meet and, contrary to the norm at the time, were also very indulgent towards their daughter, letting her explore her interests.

Despite being born with a leg dysfunction, Rubina had always held an interest in sports, which her parents encouraged. It was during the London Olympics in 2012 that Rubina found her true calling. Among all the sporting events she followed, Rubina was awestruck by the skill and accuracy at the shooting events. As she watched the 10 m air rifle event where Gagan Narang won the bronze medal, Rubina realized that this was what she wanted to do. And as if the universe was conspiring to bring her to her destination, in 2015, Gagan Narang's very own organization, Gun for Glory, showed up in Jabalpur.

Rubina started training in earnest, and her family left no stone unturned to help her. Her mother worked extra shifts to help pay for her equipment and fees, and she made it her priority to give her child the best nutrition they could afford. Rubina's father took on the responsibility of taking his daughter for coaching and made sure that her focus remained on the next tournament.

At the academy, Rubina was supported by coaches and mentors who not only helped her hone her skills, but also encouraged her to build the mental resilience that would serve her well when she decided to take the step up to the international level.

After proving herself in the domestic arena and earning a boatload of medals, Rubina decided to test international waters in 2017. This was necessary, as one of the major skills that para shooters need, especially when it comes to pistol shooting, is a steady stance. Rifle shooters, by contrast, have a supporting stand. Rubina therefore had to learn to hold her pistol steady through these contests.

After gaining some confidence and winning medals at international tournaments, Rubina's first big test came in the form of the 2018 Asian Para Games. This was her first big international tournament. She couldn't qualify for the final there, but her coaches and her parents never let her feel like she had performed badly. Her coach J.P. Nautiyal, who had also helped procure special shoes for Rubina to help her with her stance, stood by her, consoling and encouraging her. The ability to bounce back and this robust support system helped Rubina achieve the things she did.

**Rubina made history by becoming the first Indian woman to win a Paralympics medal in pistol shooting.**

The following year, at the 2019 World Shooting Para Sport World Cup in Osijek, Croatia, Rubina delivered an outstanding performance as she nabbed the bronze medal, breaking her own junior world record in the process. This would also be the final time she participated in the junior categories, with both she and her coach confident that she was ready to take the next big step.

But just as things were starting to go right for Rubina, the pandemic struck. This threw her entire preparation into a spin, as shooting ranges closed and tournaments were postponed indefinitely. Rubina had been eagerly waiting to be a part of the 2020 Paralympics, but that wait was extended by a year.

By the time the world opened up, Rubina's trigger finger was itching. The first event she took part in was the 2021 World Shooting Para Sport World Cup in Lima, which was also the last event where shooters could qualify for the Tokyo Paralympics. Rubina broke the world record as she clinched the gold. She, her family and her coaches were on top of the world when misfortune struck. Rubina caught COVID-19, and while the symptoms weren't serious, it again threw her practice off schedule as she had to quarantine for an extended period. She managed to get well and be somewhat ready by the time the Paralympics arrived, but Rubina's confidence had wavered. She managed to finish seventh, which was an achievement in itself, but she had wanted more.

Her family and her coaches did not let her wallow in the sadness of defeat. Within no time, Rubina was back on the shooting range, chasing after another dream and another medal.

In 2022, Rubina became a regular podium contender at the international level. She won the gold medal in the mixed team event at the World Shooting Para Sport Championships at Al Ain, UAE, which she followed up with a bronze at the Asian Para Championships in Hangzhou.

By the time the 2024 Paris Paralympics rolled around, nothing could stop Rubina. She won the bronze, narrowly missing out on a silver, making her the first Indian woman pistol shooter to win a medal at the Paralympics or Olympics. Of course, neither Rubina nor her coaches are satisfied with just a bronze. Watch out for her at the next Paralympics!

# *Shot Put*

INDIA
MALIK

# Deepa Malik

## F53 SHOT PUT

12 September 2016 is a landmark day in Indian sports, but most Indians might not be aware of it. And the person who made this possible will truly inspire you not just through their sporting excellence, but their outlook on living and achieving miraculous feats as well.

Deepa Malik was born in 1970 in Bengaluru. The daughter of an army officer, her upbringing exposed her to a variety of cultures and experiences, which enriched her understanding of the world and herself. But just as she was taking tentative steps into the world, Deepa was diagnosed with a tumorous growth in her spine, which needed to be surgically removed. While the operation was successful, Deepa needed a copious amount of physiotherapy to get walking again. But with a supportive family and a never-say-die attitude, Deepa made it through this ordeal and slowly got back to the activities and games she enjoyed.

Belonging to an army background, one of Deepa's biggest hobbies was travelling and biking. She was extremely invested in sports as well, but that was simply on the level of recreation till now. But as she grew, her love for motorsports increased, and Deepa dreamed of having her own bike which she could off-road and see the country in. Her soon-to-be husband, Bikram Singh Malik, was an avid biker himself, and proposed to Deepa soon after he had gotten commissioned as an officer in the army. The two got married and life seemed extremely rosy and peaceful for the couple.

However, in 1999, the spinal tumour issue which had been nipped in the bud years ago, flared up again. This time, it was more aggressive than before and Deepa had to undergo three surgeries to have it removed. The nature of the surgery and the seriousness of the tumour meant that despite physiotherapy, Deepa was not able to walk again. This would have been a serious blow to anyone, but for someone like Deepa, who loved to travel and bike, this would have hit a lot harder.

Despite these setbacks, Deepa Malik never lost her zeal for life and held on to her interests. A few years after being relegated to a wheelchair, Deepa developed a passion for sports that went a few notches above her initial interest in it. Part of it was necessitated by doctors' recommendations as well as an unwillingness to just sit around and do nothing. The first sport she picked up was swimming, which was something she had already been adept at, and it required Deepa to tweak her technique before she got comfortable with it and started winning amateur and even professional competitions left, right and centre. Her crowning achievement in the sport came at the 2006 FESPIC (Far East and South Pacific Games for the Disabled), where she won the silver. She also participated in the 2008 World Open Swimming Championships in Berlin, and to fulfil a personal dream, also swam across the Yamuna – a feat recorded in the Limca Book of Records.

Alongside swimming, Deepa also found an affinity for athletics, particularly the projectile throwing disciplines. She was a natural when it came to shot put, discus throw, and javelin. And all this Deepa Malik was achieving well into her 30s, at a time when most athletes are thinking of winding the clock down on their careers. Among her first big tournaments was the was the 2010 Commonwealth Games in Delhi, where she qualified for the shot put throw. While she did not land a medal, the experience itself would hold her in good stead and help her prepare for the windfall of podiums that was to follow.

A veteran and champion of multiple sports, Deepa has been felicitated with the Arjuna Award (2012), Padma Shri (2017), Khel Ratna (2019) and the President's Role Model Award (2014).

Participating simultaneously in discus throw, shot put and javelin throwing, Deepa needed to be able to mentally switch into different gears, which she managed superbly. At the IWAS (now World Ability Sport Games) Games in 2009, she won the bronze medal in shot put in front of a home crowd in Bengaluru. She followed this up with two more bronze medals and a new Asian record in both javelin and shot put.

In 2011, Deepa Malik switched into another gear as she took the silver in the IPC Athletics World Championships for shot put and followed it up with two golds at the Malaysian Open Athletics Championship. The Asian Para Games, where Deepa first competed and won the bronze in 2010 for javelin throw, making her the first Indian woman to win a medal there, became her stomping ground as she won four medals in three successive editions, becoming the first woman to do so. Her Asian Record in the javelin throw still stands unbroken as of 2025.

Deepa's crowning achievement came in 2016, where, at the Rio Paralympics, she won the silver in shot put at the age of forty six, making her the first ever Indian woman to win a Paralympic medal. It wasn't just the position, but the way she had achieved it, and her perseverance and determination for over fifteen years of a stellar athletic career. In recognition of her brilliance, the government has felicitated her with the Khel Ratna, as well as the Padma Shri.

A trailblazer in every sense, Deepa Malik's achievements transcend sports. Outside of athletics, her love for biking and motorsports led to her to campaign for differently abled drivers, and she was among the first people in the country to receive a license for a modified rally vehicle. As she was coming up the ranks of athletics, Deepa Malik also participated in the gruelling Raid De Himalaya and Desert Storm rally events in 2009 and 2010 respectively.

While she has since retired from active sports, Deepa Malik became the first woman to serve as the President of the Paralympic Committee of India in 2020, continuing to inspire and encourage emerging sportspersons across disciplines. Knowing the importance of mental health and resilience in sports, she has also started Wheeling Happiness, which promotes emotional and mental wellbeing among Para athletes.

A legend of Para Sports and a testament to hard work, resilience and determination, Deepa Malik is a hero in every sense of the word.

# *Swimming*

# Murlikant Petkar

## 50 M FREESTYLE SWIMMING

The 2024 Paris Paralympics saw the Indian contingent rake in medals across several disciplines. Some stars were born, others jumped into a new orbit. But few people know about the incredible story of India's very first Paralympian medallist and his legendary exploits. His is a story that seems straight out of a Bollywood movie, and indeed has been made into one too.

Murlikant Petkar was born in 1944 in a small village near Sangli, Maharashtra. His father was a freedom fighter and made a living as a tailor. Despite the family's modest means, Murlikant had a happy childhood. He and his friends would often engage in wrestling, which was the only sport popular in rural India at the time. Life in the village was full of physical exertion, something that young Murlikant grew to enjoy.

As the nation settled into independence, a new way of thinking about identity and pride was born, and Murlikant's generation was the first to embody this thinking. He had a competitive streak, and as he grew up, it became clear that the young boy's life lay outside the boundaries of the village. Murlikant left his village for the city of Pune while still in his teens.

In Pune, his physical prowess impressed recruiters in the Indian Army, and he joined as a jawan in the Corps of Electric and Mechanical Engineers (EME). Once in the army, Murlikant was exposed to every single sport possible, and he excelled at all of them. His seniors realized this and instead of regular craftsman work, Murlikant was trained as a boxer. With its similarity to wrestling, the young man took to the sport like a fish to water and mastered it. This was also the time that he became acquainted with the Olympics and made it his life's mission to win an Olympic medal for the country. By 1964, he was representing India at the International Services Sports Meet, where he came agonizingly close to winning. This only inspired Murlikant to work harder.

In 1965, war broke out between India and Pakistan, and Murlikant was deployed at the border. His unit had been camped in the Sialkot sector of Jammu and Kashmir, and one day came under a surprise aerial attack. Murlikant, who was getting his tea at that time, could barely find cover before bullets pierced his body. A total of nine bullets went in, and while the doctors were able to take out eight of them, one was embedded deep in his lower spine, which they could not take out without seriously risking Murlikant's life. The result was that he lost the use of his legs and remained in recovery for nearly two years.

This hit the young and athletic serviceman hard. Murlikant's career as a sportsperson was over. It required a lot of mental resilience and strength for him to make peace with his situation. But sports came to Murlikant's rescue here too.

During his recovery, Murlikant was prescribed many different sports to strengthen his muscles, and he excelled at them all, picking them up the way a natural athlete does. But swimming–which he'd been introduced to recently and which he was the weakest at–was a new and unknown frontier, and it challenged and intrigued him in equal measure.

Other than swimming, Murlikant also competed in the javelin throw, men's slalom and shot put in the 1972 Paralympics, reaching the finals of each discipline.

At the 1968 Paralympic Games in Tokyo, Murlikant was among India's very first contingent of ten athletes at the Games. Since swimming was still a new discipline for him, Murlikant's sport of choice was table tennis. While he cleared the first round, he was unable to advance any further. Nevertheless, by being at the Games he was able to meet so many Paralympians from across the world. This was a formative experience, much like the one he had had when he joined the army after leaving his village.

Over the next four years, Murlikant dominated whichever sport he played on the national level. He became the Maharashtra State Champion in shot put, archery, discus throw, weightlifting and table tennis. Meanwhile, he kept getting better at swimming, and despite being a champion in so many disciplines, he decided to focus on swimming, in order to become a world-class swimmer.

The 1972 Paralympics arrived, and this time Murlikant was prepared. He was competing in javelin throw, shot put, men's slalom (a timed obstacle race on a wheelchair) and swimming. Murlikant easily made it to the final round of each event, and the small contingent of ten athletes believed that he would manage to get on the podium.

By winning the gold medal in the 50 m men's freestyle event, Murlikant became the first Indian to win an individual medal at either the Olympics or the Paralympics. He also broke the world record with his attempt of 37.33 seconds. Everyone present at the event was shocked to see the medal go to a country that is not known for its swimmers, or even athletes outside of hockey. But Murlikant Petkar had done it; he had put India on the world map.

However, due to the lack of television screens and a general lack of interest in sports, Murlikant did not get the kind of adulation he deserved at home. It was only in 2017 that authorities and journalists rediscovered the story of this forgotten gem of India. In recognition of his achievements, Murlikant Petkar was awarded the Padma Shri in 2018, nearly fifty years after his crowning moment, and the Arjuna Award in 2024. His is the kind of inspirational story you don't come across very often.

# *Table Tennis*

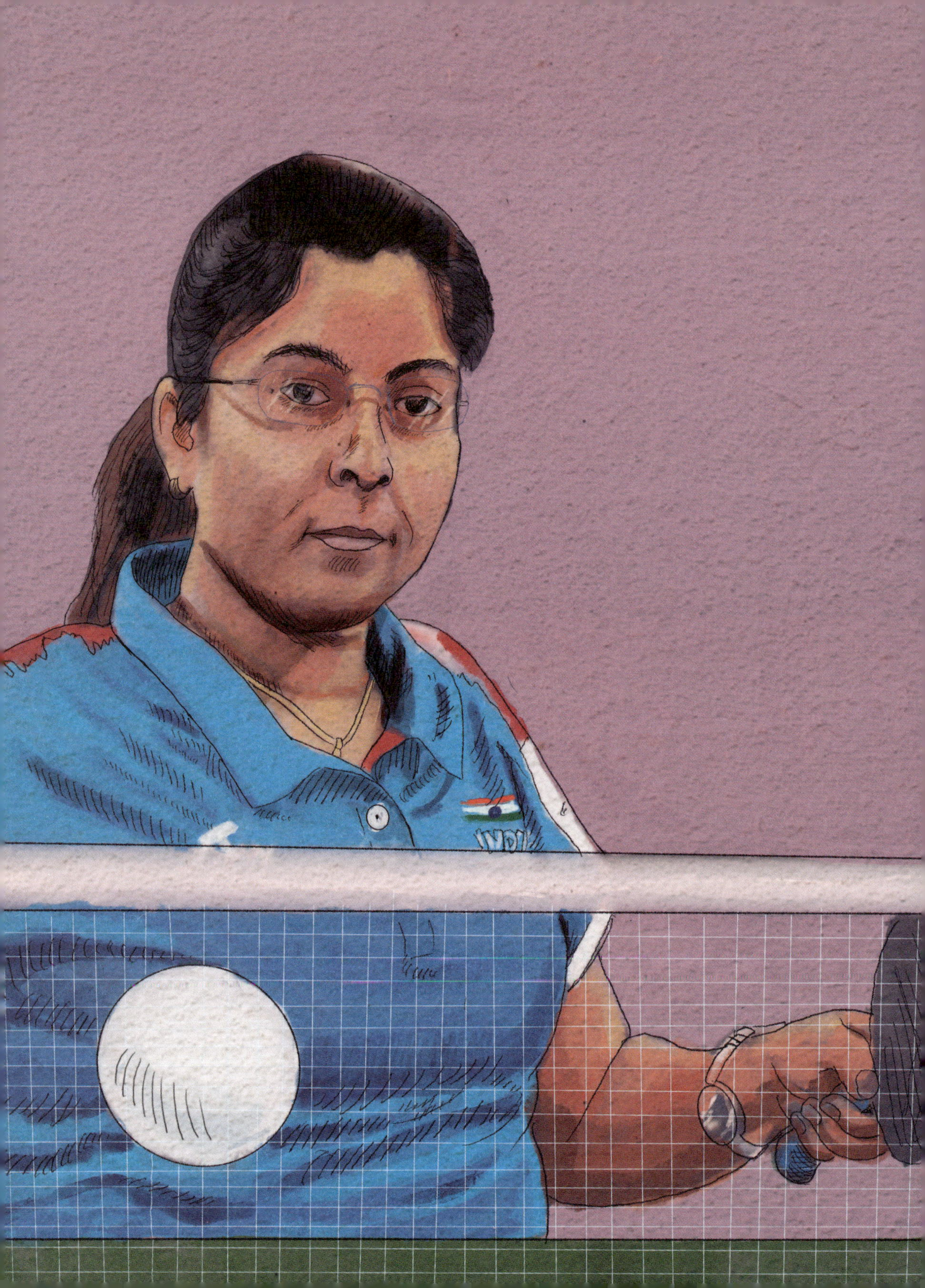

## Bhavina Patel

### C4 TABLE TENNIS

As the competitor stood on the second step of the podium and the ceremony got underway, she couldn't help but think about all that had happened in the past few days. The sheer joy of winning, the disappointment of losing and the wishes and praise she had received had been a bit too much to comprehend in such a short time. But now, she took it all in. She remembered for a second the pain of four years ago, and her eyes misted over. But that was a distant memory, and she was here, in Tokyo, after one extra year, basking in glory.

Bhavina Patel was born in Mehsana, a historical town in Gujarat, in 1986. Her father ran a small snack shop in Vadnagar Tehsil village in Mehsana, while her mother worked part time. Things got tough for the family when Bhavina was diagnosed with polio at the tender age of one and lost the use of her legs as a result. But her parents tried to provide for her in whatever way they could.

Bhavina was a docile and obedient child, and enjoyed spending time with books. However, being wheelchair-bound often gave rise to frustration and she thoroughly detested it when her family had to help her do even basic tasks like moving around or getting ready for school. She wanted to change this, wanted to be independent.

Bhavina's interest in academics led her to enrol in an IT course at the Blind People's Association in Ahmedabad alongside pursuing her graduation through correspondence. There, Bhavina fell in love with something she never thought would happen. Having made friends at the campus, she saw how much they enjoyed playing table tennis. Bhavina was vaguely familiar with the sport, but once she got a taste of it, she was drawn in. Her family was surprised at her newfound passion but decided to support her interest.

This was a time when para sports were not a part of public imagination and lacked adequate funding, even after Devendra Jhajharia's record-breaking gold medal at the Athens Paralympics. Gujarat, specifically, was not known for its athletes outside of cricket. Despite this, Bhavina persevered, training day and night for three years before feeling ready to participate in the National Championships. While most participants had coaches and instructors, Bhavina was going at it solo, with only the support of her family and friends.

At her first National Championships, Bhavina won the bronze medal. It was at this point that she first considered becoming a professional athlete. More than the medal, though, the event brought her into contact with Lalan Doshi, who would become her coach and help her take her game to the next level.

By the time the Commonwealth Games rolled around in 2010, everyone knew Bhavina and her game. She was heralded as one of India's top medal hopes at the Games that were being held in Delhi. Unfortunately, Bhavina fell short at the quarterfinals, forcing her to go back to the drawing board. She relentlessly studied her game, almost like a student. Her dedicated academic approach led her to rigorously analyze her technique and style, which included poring over videos of her previous matches with her coach, as well as observing the movement and shot selection of her opponents.

**Bhavina became the first para athlete from Gujarat to win a medal, and the first Indian to win a Paralympics medal in table tennis.**

This analytical approach propelled Bhavina to the rank of world number two, and on to the podium at various tournaments. The Asian scene, which was one of the most competitive when it came to table tennis, had Bhavina mixing it up with the Chinese paddlers, considered the best in the world, and she often ended up defeating them with ease.

Bhavina was all set when the 2016 Rio Paralympics arrived, raring to go and show the world her mastery of the game. To help her get new equipment, facilities and everything else she needed for the trip, her parents took a loan and sold their snack shop. Everything seemed to be in place for an epic tournament.

But owing to a small technicality arising out of a delay in paperwork, Bhavina could not participate in this edition. It happened at the last moment, and it broke her heart. While she was certainly dejected at the thought of not competing, she felt worse for her parents, and the loan that now had to be repaid. Nevertheless, her family, including her husband Nikul Patel, a sportsperson himself, helped Bhavina bounce back from the setback. Gradually, the loan was repaid, and Bhavina put the disappointment behind her and got working with her coach again.

Before the Tokyo Paralympics five years later, Bhavina went to Ahmedabad to start preparing for the event. Her parents accompanied her there so that she could concentrate on her training. As she left for Japan, Bhavina promised that she would come back with a medal.

Her first-round match, where she was up against the world number one Zhou Ying, did not go as per plan, and Bhavina lost in straight games. But she put the defeat, like the countless others she had encountered over the years, at the back of her mind. She won straight games after that, going all the way to the final undefeated, beating players much younger and higher ranked than her.

At the finals, Bhavina was up against Zhou Ying again. While she lost the match, she had already attained immortality, having become the very first Indian paddler to win a medal at the Paralympics, as well as the first Gujarati person to win a medal at either the Paralympics or the Olympics. A year later, she fulfilled the very first dream she had had as a professional as well, winning the gold at the Commonwealth Games in 2022.

Still competing at the highest level at the age of thirty-eight, Bhavina shows no sign of stopping anytime soon.

# Track

PAL

# Preethi Pal

## T35 100 M AND 200 M

Most of the athletes you've read about so far have primarily competed in either field or indoor events. India has struggled at track events throughout its sporting history. Apart from a few instances, Indian racers haven't quite been able to make a mark like the javelin throwers and shooters. That is, until 2024, when a girl showed the country how it was done.

Preethi Pal was born in 2000 in Hashampur, a small village near Muzaffarnagar. The daughter of a dairy farmer, Preethi was the second girl child in the family. The family eventually had two boys, but Preethi, while loved by her family, was often scorned by the village folk. In addition to being female, Preethi was also born with cerebral palsy, causing her to have deformed feet, which just added to the constant barbs aimed at her. To try and curtail the deformity, her legs were put in casts for months right after her birth, which, instead of helping things, made them worse.

Being from a poor, rural background, Preethi's parents tried every quack remedy available to them, but to no avail. The ceaseless experimenting had an adverse effect on the child's immunity, and she became sickly as a result. Eventually, her parents gave up and got Preethi callipers to help her stand by herself and walk without pain.

By the time she was of school-going age, Preethi and her siblings were sent to live with their grandparents in Meerut. While this was a welcome change for Preethi as she didn't have to listen to the villagers' taunts anymore, it was still a tough time. She had to babysit her brothers, as well as cook food and do other household chores early every morning. But she didn't complain and got on with her work alongside her schooling.

At school, Preethi found her vocation. More than studies, she was interested in sports. One would think that a girl with callipers would be ill-suited to sports, but that was not the case. Preethi's condition meant that while she struggled to stand straight due to her heels, she had taught herself, unconsciously, to walk on her toes. This meant that while running, she had a much more natural posture than she did while standing or walking. Preethi would just take the callipers off in front of her classmates and beat them hands down at every race. It surprised people that a girl who struggled to walk and had this unusual gait ran like greased lightning.

As the school years rolled on, Preethi's ambitions took shape. Here was an activity that she could do better than her able-bodied peers. And so, while she took care of housework and her studies, Preethi also began looking for a way to become a professional athlete. During her research, Preethi ran into para athlete Fatima Khatoon, who opened her eyes to an entire world of possibilities.

It was the first time Preethi had seen para athletes in her life. And when she learnt about the Paralympics, her dreams soared even higher. She saw blade runners competing in races and winning medals and drew inspiration from them. She started training in earnest, taking help and tips from Khatoon, who supported her in every way she could.

For becoming the first Indian track athlete to win two Paralympic medals, the Arjuna Award was conferred on Preethi in 2024.

But as soon as she started competing at the national level, the pandemic struck. Preethi's father's dairy business started faltering, and she had to help out at home a lot more than she used to. But thankfully, her siblings were all grown up now, so as soon as the lockdown ended, Preethi got back to training.

One of the things that limited Preethi—as does a lot of Indian athletes in general—is diet. While lack of facilities can be made up for by alternative training methods, a nutritious diet is paramount for a young athlete to grow and succeed. Preethi struggled to maintain a diet that included the occasional fruit if she could afford it. Seeing this, Khatoon introduced her to Gajendra Singh, a coach, whose wife, Simran Sharma, is among India's best para runners. Gajendra Singh saw promise but set the condition that Preethi would never say no to training if she wanted him to coach her. Relocating to Delhi, Preethi fell into this new routine with vigour.

After winning medals in the national championships, Preethi's international debut came at the Asian Para Championships in 2023. There, despite a spirited attempt, she finished fourth in both the 100 m and 200 m sprints. That she had missed out on a medal by a whisker was devastating for Preethi. But the support system of her coach and fellow para athletes helped her bounce back and keep her dream in sight.

The year after, Preethi won two golds at the Indian Open Para Athletics Championships, which put her in a good frame of mind for the World Para Athletics Championships in Kobe. This time, with a much bigger field of competition, Preethi won the bronze in both the 100 m and the 200 m sprints. But she wasn't done yet. The big test was to come in only a few months, and Preethi couldn't even take time off and celebrate.

At the 2024 Paris Paralympics, Preethi won bronze medals in the same categories she had at the Kobe Games, becoming the first Indian track athlete to win a medal at either the Paralympics or the Olympics, and also the first Indian woman to win two medals in track and field. She celebrated with her coach and Simran Sharma at the Eiffel Tower, taking in the grand monument, and promising to go for the gold the next time.

# Know More ...

Artistic sports are those that combine athleticism with grace and precision-based skills, like figure skating, diving, rhythmic gymnastics and equestrian sports. Out of these, para equestrian dressage is the only artistic discipline at the Paralympics so far. Consisting of various aids and equipments specific to para athletes, para dressage requires oodles of discipline from both athlete and the horse. It is also a gender neutral event, with athletes in a similar classification competing against each other.

INDIA
DEEVANJI

## Deepthi Jeevanji

**T20 400 M**

Overnight, India went from being a field specialist in athletics to becoming a strong competitor on the running track as well. All this was down to two women specializing in different disciplines. While Preethi Pal earned plaudits for her sprinting, the other medal winner is a testament to endurance and unending patience with her legendary exploits at medium distance running. Journeying from a small rural setting to prestigious international podiums with her prodigious pace, this runner has redefined the very meaning of luck through her skill.

Deepthi Jeevanji was born in Kellada, a small village in Telangana, in 2003. As she was born during an eclipse, the villagers declared that there was something wrong with the child, dooming her in their eyes. When it became apparent that she also had an intellectual disability, making it difficult for her to communicate and understand complex concepts easily, the villagers decided that it would be best if the family gave up the girl for adoption, or got her admitted in an asylum.

Deepthi's parents were farmers and daily wage labourers who tilled their own half-acre land alongside helping out on other people's farms. With limited education and exposure, her parents seriously considered giving Deepthi up, since they had one more mouth to feed in her younger sister. But they eventually realized that their child was special, and that the eclipse had not been a curse, but a boon.

Unfortunately, the rest of the village did not share this belief. The young Deepthi, barely five, was berated and mocked ceaselessly by her peers and even their parents. Her only impulse would be to run home and cry copiously. Her mother would placate her by giving her either curd rice or chicken, both of which Deepthi loved to eat. Gradually, she joined a school in Warangal and had to contend with even more bullying. But Deepthi did not lose heart.

A healthy diet and an active lifestyle which included helping with household chores, gave Deepthi an athletic build from childhood. Running became her sanctuary, because it was the only time she didn't hear the taunts of other kids and her fellow students. But even her miraculous speed, though undisputed, was not enough to spare Deepthi the insults of most people she came across.

Then, in 2018, during a sports meet at her school, Deepthi was spotted by someone who believed in her ability and saw the brilliance she was capable of. This was N. Ramesh, a coach with the Sports Authority of India. Sure that he had finally discovered one of India's first running superstars, Ramesh asked Deepthi's family to send her to Hyderabad. When they responded that they did not have enough money to send her on the 130-kilometre journey from Warangal, Ramesh took matters into his own hands and arranged her conveyance. From that early moment, the coach had full faith in his charge, someone he hadn't even started coaching yet.

Deepthi broke the world record (55.06s) at the 2024 World Championships in Kobe en route to her historic gold.

But this was all repaid when Deepthi turned up for training. An eager student, she was respectful towards her coaches and the staff, always listening to their guidance and advice. Her coaches were equally receptive towards this ideal student, taking time out for her and carefully explaining to her concepts that she had trouble grasping.

After a year of strenuous training, Deepthi's coaches felt that she was ready for the big leagues. Her first competition was the 2019 Asian Youth Championships in Hong Kong. It was Deepthi's first time at such a large stadium, and among such crowds. Yet, she did not let the occasion get to her as she marked her competitive debut with a bronze medal.

Now that she got a taste of the podium, Deepthi didn't look back. She had found the thing she wanted to do, and which made her and those around her happy. The year after, she participated in the Khelo India Youth Games, where she swept aside the competition en route to winning two golds in both the 100 m and 200 m events.

By the time 2022 rolled around, Deepthi had become one of the most recognizable and formidable runners in India. The only goal now was to make her a household name. At the 2022 Hangzhou Asian Para Games, held in 2023, Deepthi was selected as part of the Indian team to make her senior debut on the track. Although she was comfortable running any distance, her favoured event was the 400 m, which made use of all her explosive strength as well as patience to conserve energy. As expected, she won the gold, and on the way to that, broke the Asian record as well as the Games record, clocking an impressive 56.69s, shocking those who had yet to hear of her brilliance.

If anyone thought this was a flash in the pan, Deepthi decided to outperform herself the year after. At the World Para Athletics Championships in Kobe, she broke the world record, setting the new one at 55.07s, an entire half second faster than her previous best. She again set a new Asian record later in the year with a 56.18s, which automatically qualified her for the Paralympics, an event that she had been dreaming about ever since she had decided to run professionally.

At the 2024 Paris Paralympics, Deepthi became the second Indian woman, after Preethi Pal in the same edition, to win a medal for India in track, winning the bronze in 400 m with relative ease. As her family, coaches, and even the village that had vilified her at such a young age celebrated, Deepthi looked on with pride and unbridled joy. But this journey has just started and the young sprinter has been earmarked for a future Paralympic gold.

# India's Paralympic Medallists

India has had consistent representation in the Paralympics since 1968, with the size of its contingent increasing every edition and bringing laurels to the country. Since 1968, Indian para athletes have won a total of 60 medals across various sports and disciplines. In chronological order, starting with the legendary Murlikant Petkar, here is a comprehensive list of India's Paralympics medallists.

1. Murlikant Petkar: Gold, 50 m Freestyle Swimming (1972 Heidelberg, West Germany)
2. Bhimrao Kesarkar: Silver, Men's Javelin L6 (1984 New York, USA)
3. Joginder Singh Bedi: Silver, Men's Shot Put L6. Bronze, Men's Javelin L6 and Men's Discus Throw L6 (1984 New York, USA)
4. Devendra Jhajharia: Gold, Men's Javelin F42–46 (2004 Athens, Greece). Gold, Men's Javelin F46 (2016 Rio de Janeiro, Brazil). Silver, Men's Javelin F46 (2020 Tokyo, Japan)
5. Rajinder Singh Rahelu: Bronze, Powerlifting Men's 56kg (2004 Athens, Greece)
6. Girisha Nagarajegowda: Silver, Men's High Jump T42 (2012 London, UK)
7. Mariyappan Thangavelu: Gold, Men's High Jump T42 (2016 Rio de Janeiro, Brazil). Silver, Men's High Jump T63 (2020 Tokyo, Japan). Bronze, Men's High Jump T63 (2024 Paris, France)
8. Deepa Malik: Silver, Women's Shot Put F53 (2016 Rio de Janeiro, Brazil)

9. Varun Singh Bhati: Bronze, Men's High Jump T42 (2016 Rio de Janeiro, Brazil)
10. Avani Lekhara: Gold, Women's 10 m Air Rifle SH1 (2020 Tokyo, Japan). Bronze, Women's 50 m Air Rifle SH1 (2020 Tokyo, Japan). Gold, Women's 10 m Air Rifle SH1 (2024 Paris, France)
11. Manish Narwal: Gold, Men's 50 m Air Pistol SH1 (2020 Tokyo, Japan). Silver, Men's 10 m Air Pistol SH1 (2024 Paris, France)
12. Sumit Antil: Gold, Men's Javelin F64 (2020 Tokyo, Japan). Gold, Men's Javelin F64 (2024 Paris, France)
13. Pramod Bhagat: Gold, Men's Badminton SL3 (2020 Tokyo, Japan).
14. Krishna Nagar: Gold, Men's Badminton SH6 (2020 Tokyo, Japan).
15. Bhavina Patel: Silver, Women's Table Tennis C4 (2020 Tokyo, Japan).
16. Nishad Kumar: Silver, Men's High Jump T47 (2020 Tokyo, Japan). Silver, Men's High Jump T47 (2024 Paris, France).
17. Yogesh Kathuniya: Silver, Men's Discus Throw F56 (2020 Tokyo, Japan). Silver, Men's Discus Throw F56 (2024 Paris, France)
18. Praveen Kumar: Silver, Men's High Jump T64 (2020 Tokyo, Japan). Gold, Men's High Jump T64 (2024 Paris, France)
19. Singhraj Adhana: Silver, Men's 50 m Air Pistol SH1 (2020 Tokyo, Japan). Bronze, Men's 10 m Air Pistol SH1 (2020 Tokyo, Japan)
20. Suhas Yathiraj: Silver, Men's Badminton SL4 (2020 Tokyo, Japan). Silver, Men's Badminton SL4 (2024 Paris, France)
21. Sundar Singh Gurjar: Bronze, Men's Javelin F46 (2020 Tokyo, Japan). Bronze, Men's Javelin F46 (2024 Paris, France)
22. Sharad Kumar: Bronze, Men's High Jump T63 (2020 Tokyo, Japan). Silver, Men's High Jump T63 (2024 Paris, France)
23. Harvinder Singh: Bronze, Men's Recurve Archery (2020 Tokyo, Japan). Gold, Men's Recurve Archery (2024 Paris, France)

24. Manoj Sarkar: Bronze, Men's Badminton SL3 (2020 Tokyo, Japan)
25. Nitesh Kumar: Gold, Men's Badminton SL3 (2024 Paris, France)
26. Dharambir Nain: Gold, Men's Club Throw F51 (2024 Paris, France)
27. Navdeep Singh: Gold, Men's Javelin F41 (2024 Paris, France)
28. Thulasimathi Murugesan: Silver, Women's Badminton SU5 (2024 Paris, France)
29. Ajeet Singh Yadav: Silver, Men's Javelin F46 (2024 Paris, France)
30. Sachin Khilari: Silver, Men's Shot Put F46 (2024 Paris, France)
31. Pranav Soorma: Silver, Men's Club Throw F51 (2024 Paris, France)
32. Preethi Pal: Bronze, Women's 100 m T35 (2024 Paris, France). Bronze, Women's 200 m T35 (2024 Paris, France)
33. Mona Agarwal: Bronze, Women's 10 m Air Rifle SH1 (2024 Paris, France)
34. Rubina Francis: Bronze, Women's 10 m Air Pistol SH1 (2024 Paris, France)
35. Manisha Ramadass: Bronze, Women's Badminton SU5 (2024 Paris, France)
36. Nithya Sre Sivan: Bronze, Women's Badminton SH6 (2024 Paris, France)
37. Sheetal Devi: Bronze, Mixed Team Compound Archery (2024 Paris, France)
38. Rakesh Kumar: Bronze, Mixed Team Compound Archery (2024 Paris, France)
39. Deepthi Jeevanji: Bronze, Women's 400 m T20 (2024 Paris, France)
40. Simran Sharma: Bronze, Women's 200 m T12 (2024 Paris, France)
41. Hokato Hotozhe Sema: Bronze, Men's Shot Put F57 (2024 Paris, France)
42. Kapil Parmar: Bronze, Men's Judo J1 60 kg (2024 Paris, France)

# About the Illustrator

Mistunee Chowdhury is a Delhi-based illustrator, animator, painter and sculpture artist. Trained in and employing a wide variety of media, she has done caricatures and illustrated for picture books, comics, story books for HarperCollins, NBT, Hachette India, Scholastic and others.

# Other Sports Biographies by HarperCollins

*What did it take for Neeraj Chopra to perform at the world stage for the first time? What obstacles did Mary Kom surmount before reaching the winner's podium? What challenges did Annu Rani face and how did she overcome them to achieve victory?*

*Golden Sportspersons* is a compilation of the inspiring tales of India's legendary sportspersons, who have shone in archery, athletics, badminton, boxing, chess, cricket, football, gymnastics, hockey, shooting, weightlifting and wrestling. The collection in this book includes sporting legends such as Karnam Malleswari, Neeraj Chopra, Deepika Kumari, Sachin Tendulkar, Annu Rani, Bhaichung Bhutia, Mirabai Chanu, P.V. Sindhu, and many others, whose lives are worth emulating.

*Who is the first Indian to become a number 1 ranked badminton player? Who is the only cricket captain to win all three ICC Trophies? Can you name the first footballer to reach 100 career wins in the UEFA Champions League?*

Find out the answers to these questions and more in *Goal, Shot, Run!* A collection of illustrated biographies of sportspeople from all over the world. From cricket to hockey, tennis to football and even the Olympics, it's time to learn more about your favourite sports superstars, and maybe even discover some new ones!

Short, snappy information from their birthdate to where they live, the awards they've won, their first game and more, accompanied by colourful illustrations. This is a quick and easy-to-read fan guide.

Featured personalities include Cristiano Ronaldo, Dipa Karmakar, Leander Paes, Lionel Messi, Mary Kom, PV Sindhu, Serena Williams, Virat Kohli and many more!

# Other Timeless Biographies by HarperCollins

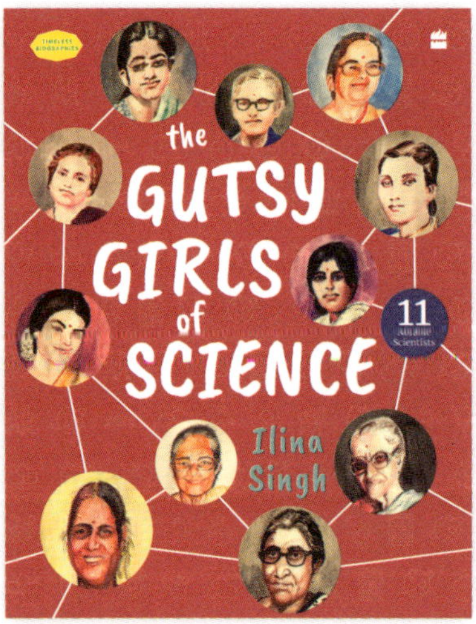


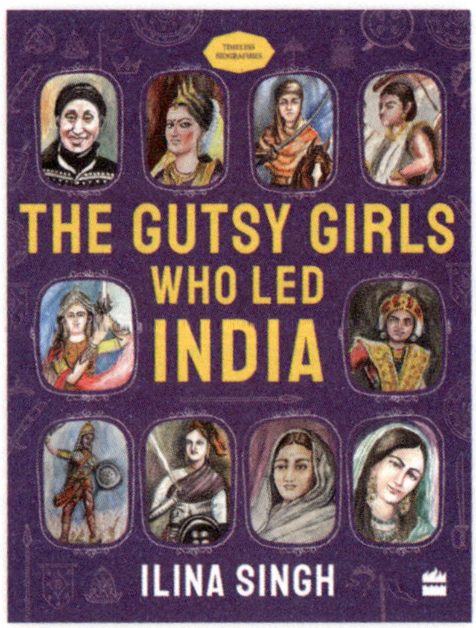

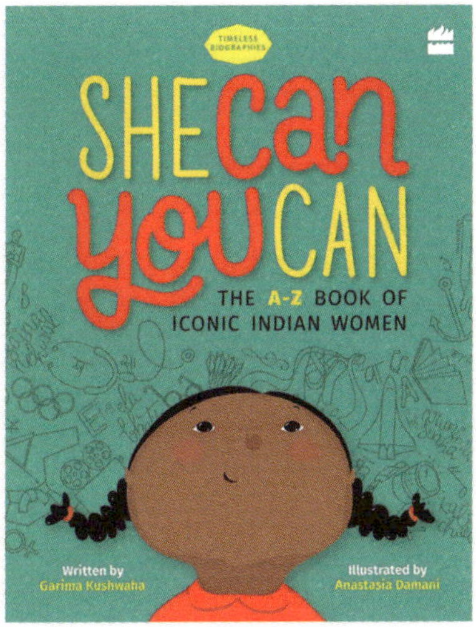
TIMELESS BIOGRAPHIES
SHE CAN YOU CAN
THE A-Z BOOK OF ICONIC INDIAN WOMEN
Written by
Garima Kushwaha
Illustrated by
Anastasia Damani

TIMELESS BIOGRAPHIES
A Star Named Bibha and Other Stories
Anwesha Sengupta
Supurna Banerjee
Simantini Mukhopadhyay